Nation-Building

Other Books of Related Interest:

Opposing Viewpoints Series

Afghanistan

America's Global Influence

Iran

North & South Korea

Rogue Nations

At Issue Series

Can Democracy Succeed in the Middle East?

Can the War on Terrorism Be Won?

Is Iran a Threat to Global Security?

Current Controversies Series

Afghanistan

Developing Nations

"Congress shall make
no law ... abridging
the freedom of speech,
or of the press."

First Amendment to the U.S. Constitution

The basic foundation of our democracy is the First Amendment guarantee of freedom of expression. The Opposing Viewpoints series is dedicated to the concept of this basic freedom and the idea that it is more important to practice it than to enshrine it.

OPPOSING VIEWPOINTS® SERIES

Nation-Building

Michael Logan, Book Editor

GREENHAVEN PRESS

An imprint of Thomson Gale, a part of The Thomson Corporation

Detroit • New York • San Francisco • New Haven, Conn. • Waterville, Maine • London

Christine Nasso, *Publisher*
Elizabeth Des Chenes, *Managing Editor*

© 2007 The Gale Group.

Star logo is a trademark and Gale and Greenhaven Press are registered trademarks used herein under license.

For more information, contact:
Greenhaven Press
27500 Drake Rd.
Farmington Hills, MI 48331-3535
Or you can visit our Internet site at http://www.gale.com

Cover photograph reproduced by permission of photos.com.

LIBRARY OF CONGRESS CATALOGING-IN-PUBLICATION DATA

Nation-building / Michael Logan, book editor.
    p. cm. -- (Opposing viewpoints)
Includes bibliographical references and index.
ISBN-13: 978-0-7377-3894-0 (hardcover)
ISBN-13: 978-0-7377-3895-7 (pbk.)
1. Nation-building. I. Logan, Michael, 1956-
JZ6300.N382 2008
355.02'8--dc22

                                                            2007024139

ISBN-10: 0-7377-3894-4 (hardcover)
ISBN-10: 0-7377-3895-2 (pbk.)

Printed in the United States of America
10 9 8 7 6 5 4 3 2 1

Contents

Chapter 3: Can Nation-Building in Iraq Work?

Chapter 4: Can Nation-Building Succeed in the 21st Century?

Why Consider Opposing Viewpoints?

"The only way in which a human being can make some approach to knowing the whole of a subject is by hearing what can be said about it by persons of every variety of opinion and studying all modes in which it can be looked at by every character of mind. No wise man ever acquired his wisdom in any mode but this."

John Stuart Mill

In our media-intensive culture it is not difficult to find differing opinions. Thousands of newspapers and magazines and dozens of radio and television talk shows resound with differing points of view. The difficulty lies in deciding which opinion to agree with and which "experts" seem the most credible. The more inundated we become with differing opinions and claims, the more essential it is to hone critical reading and thinking skills to evaluate these ideas. Opposing Viewpoints books address this problem directly by presenting stimulating debates that can be used to enhance and teach these skills. The varied opinions contained in each book examine many different aspects of a single issue. While examining these conveniently edited opposing views, readers can develop critical thinking skills such as the ability to compare and contrast authors' credibility, facts, argumentation styles, use of persuasive techniques, and other stylistic tools. In short, the Opposing Viewpoints series is an ideal way to attain the higher-level thinking and reading skills so essential in a culture of diverse and contradictory opinions.

In addition to providing a tool for critical thinking, Opposing Viewpoints books challenge readers to question their own strongly held opinions and assumptions. Most people form their opinions on the basis of upbringing, peer pressure, and personal, cultural, or professional bias. By reading carefully balanced opposing views, readers must directly confront new ideas as well as the opinions of those with whom they disagree. This is not to simplistically argue that everyone who reads opposing views will—or should—change his or her opinion. Instead, the series enhances readers' understanding of their own views by encouraging confrontation with opposing ideas. Careful examination of others' views can lead to the readers' understanding of the logical inconsistencies in their own opinions, perspective on why they hold an opinion, and the consideration of the possibility that their opinion requires further evaluation.

Evaluating Other Opinions

To ensure that this type of examination occurs, Opposing Viewpoints books present all types of opinions. Prominent spokespeople on different sides of each issue as well as well-known professionals from many disciplines challenge the reader. An additional goal of the series is to provide a forum for other, less-known, or even unpopular viewpoints. The opinion of an ordinary person who has had to make the decision to cut off life support from a terminally ill relative, for example, may be just as valuable and provide just as much insight as a medical ethicist's professional opinion. The editors have two additional purposes in including these less-known views. One, the editors encourage readers to respect others' opinions—even when not enhanced by professional credibility. It is only by reading or listening to and objectively evaluating others' ideas that one can determine whether they are worthy of consideration. Two, the inclusion of such viewpoints encourages the important critical thinking skill of objectively evaluating an author's credentials and bias. This evaluation will illuminate an author's reasons for taking a particular stance on an issue and will aid in readers' evaluation of the author's ideas.

It is our hope that these books will give readers a deeper understanding of the issues debated and an appreciation of the complexity of even seemingly simple issues when good and honest people disagree. This awareness is particularly important in a democratic society such as ours in which people enter into public debate to determine the common good. Those with whom one disagrees should not be regarded as enemies but rather as people whose views deserve careful examination and may shed light on one's own.

Thomas Jefferson once said that "difference of opinion leads to inquiry, and inquiry to truth." Jefferson, a broadly educated man, argued that "if a nation expects to be ignorant and free . . . it expects what never was and never will be." As individuals and as a nation, it is imperative that we consider the opinions of others and examine them with skill and discernment. The Opposing Viewpoints series is intended to help readers achieve this goal.

David L. Bender and Bruno Leone,
Founders

Introduction

> *"Nation-building is not for the faint-hearted."*
>
> —Michael O'Hanlon,
> Senior Foreign Policy Studies Fellow,
> the Brookings Institute

Fred Cuny disappeared in Chechnya, the war-torn region of Russia decimated by the Soviet Army, that stubbornly seeks its independence at the cost of a humanitarian and civic crisis few places in the world match. It was the cost of disasters like Chechnya that Cuny sought to minimize because cost, for him, always translated into lives. Cuny had seen it the world over in war and natural disaster zones: the intense desire of indigenous peoples to return and rebuild their homeland.

Fred Cuny was a legend in the humanitarian assistance world made up of nongovernmental organizations (NGOs), failed states, United Nations and Western government interventions, foreign aid, and private businesses that work in disaster relief areas. An ex-marine, Cuny founded Intertect Relief and Reconstruction Services, a Dallas-based company specializing in global relief efforts. Intertect was known for its speed and efficiency in disaster stabilization and reconstruction. Its leader had a reputation as a maverick whose ideas often clashed with existing models for disaster response and rebuilding. At first, other aid organizations and governments scoffed at Cuny's methods, but as his achievements became validated globally, they began to copy him.

He was not afraid to use the black market to buy essential food and tools for victims of failed and war-torn states. Cuny thought importing tents, though it made donors feel good, was useless. He believed people should scavenge within rubble for bricks, wood, and steel for material to reconstruct their homes, instead of hauling it away prior to rebuilding. During the siege of Sarajevo (the capital of Yugoslavia) in 1993 in the Bosnian–Serbian war, Cuny directed city residents, who had no method of heating for winter, to tap into the Russian natural gas line that formerly supplied the city. Under Cuny's direction, aid groups supplied thousands of feet of plastic pipe and directed neighborhoods to dig trenches. They taught residents how to tap into the gas line and bury it. Because the Serbians surrounding the city needed gas also, Cuny knew they would not shut down the line. Under the rules of most foreign assistance programs, this would have been declared "taking sides" and would have been prohibited. Cuny only saw people who would freeze in winter and would not have the strength to rebuild their city.

He also devised a system that imported thousands of tons of seeds into Sarajevo during the winter. Residents planted them in backyards and balconies. By summer the city had an abundant supply of fresh produce, and residents were able to preserve and can the extra for the coming year's winter. Cuny organized the construction of an interim water system that provided precious drinking water to a city whose infrastructure had been destroyed by the siege. In an arena where Serbian sniper fire and artillery shelling were daily occurrences, he performed minor miracles of engineering and stabilization. Cuny's methods were unorthodox, but clearly he got things done.

Fred Cuny was performing nation-building. He made realistic assessments of the ground conditions where he operated. He was flexible and thought "outside the box." An intervention model for Haiti, he knew, might not work in rebuilding Zaire. He would work with warlords, persons of dubious character, United Nations representatives and peacekeepers, setting up meetings where people who would never have met—in fact, would probably have resented each other—turned toward the goal of saving and rebuilding destroyed regions. For this he was sometimes resented.

"If we throw junk aid at a problem, there won't be any impact, even if it might soothe someone's conscience, especially donors," he said. "If you just give people a tent, what does that tell them? Either you don't want them on that land or this isn't the solution. You slow down reconstruction and create expectations you can't meet. But if you give them a tool and some basic materials the message is, 'Get on with it. Let's get this thing over with. Let's rebuild the community.'"

Some of Cuny's methods challenged existing presuppositions about intervention and nation-building. For instance, he believed state sovereignty, the right of a nation to manage internal crisis situations based on its own values, morals, and laws, was an excuse used by outside nations and agencies not to intervene in crisis situations until it was too late. "We've got to get beyond this idea of strict neutrality. We've got to say, if people are in harm's way, we've got to get them out of there. The first and most important thing is saving lives. Whatever it takes to save lives, you do it, and the heck with national sovereignty. There's a higher responsibility."

Cuny harassed the United Nations and its officials for what he perceived as its many failures in nation-building and peacekeeping operations. He devised Intertect's operations on the assumption no international aid would arrive. Plan for the worst-case scenario, he advised, be self-sufficient, and create a way for the people you are helping to be self-sufficient. He thought international aid or assistance beyond worst-case scenarios needed to be closely examined for usefulness in constructing secure nation-building environments.

Intertect and Cuny raised many of the questions that are being asked of nation-building operations in Afghanistan, Iraq, Haiti, and the United Democratic Republic of Congo, to name a few. Can nation-building operate successfully in regions where insurgencies and wars continue? The viewpoints in Chapter Three of this anthology ask this question in regard to the U.S. and allied occupation of Iraq. Can nation-building be transplanted from a democratic country into religiously oriented, chaotic states? Chapter Four shares differing viewpoints on the question of whether nation-building can succeed in the 21st century, under these and other conditions. Can nation-building be justified when one country intervenes upon the national sovereignty of another? Chapter Two provides opposing viewpoints on whether nation-building is justified in terms of sovereignty and other issues. Can a similar model of nation-building succeed in Iraq and Afghanistan with their dissimilar ethnic populations and cultures? Can nation-building succeed in combating global terrorism when populations and cultures are thrown into chaos as a result of outside interventions? Chapter One seeks answers between parties with dissimilar views on the issue.

OPPOSING
VIEWPOINTS®
SERIES

CHAPTER 1

Is Nation-Building Justified?

Chapter Preface

Nation-building analysts of all persuasions consistently point to the post-World War II reconstruction of Germany and Japan from utter devastation as models of successfully rebuilt nations. From that starting point, they disagree on methods and justifications for when and where to nation-build, but the vast majority agree on the success of post-World War II reconstruction as the context for their arguments. But what if their initial premise is wrong? The question of justifying nation-building, then, becomes more chaotic, in search of new ideas and knowledge.

James L. Payne has taught political science at Johns Hopkins University and is now an independent analyst and author. His mostly solitary voice argues that the United States did a poor job of rebuilding Germany. In fact, he maintains, if the United States is searching for models that could apply to Afghanistan and Iraq, the reconstruction of Germany after 1945 is not a good choice.

Following the end of World War II, a great deal of Central Europe was devastated by the battles that had been waged across its landscape. The United States is historically congratulated for implementing the Marshall Plan, post-World War II. Named after George C. Marshall, secretary of state under Franklin Roosevelt, the goal was to aid the reconstruction of Central Europe into functioning democratic societies modeled on the United States, and to prevent the extension of communism that the Soviet Union, an ally during the war, wished to spread beyond its borders. The clash of democracy and communism after the war led to the Cold War, a battle for global dominance between the United States and Russia from 1945 to 1991. Historians commonly state that the Marshall Plan rebuilt Europe and prevented communism from taking root on the continent.

The United States developed the Marshall Plan after U.S. military forces already occupied parts of Germany (the country was divided into occupied sectors between Russian, American, and Great Britain militaries; it would ultimately be a divided country, east and west Germany, Communist and democratic, until the fall of the Berlin Wall in 1992) and all of Japan. Payne argues the U.S. Army initially worked *against* reconstructing Germany. For instance, the U.S. Joint Chiefs of Staff for military affairs, in a directive of 1945, ordered the occupiers not to collaborate with Germans. The policy was eventually abandoned, but not before, Payne notes, it created a mood of tension between occupiers and occupied. American administrators and military, in many instances, took the best houses and hotels for living quarters, pushing Germans into homelessness. Military orders prohibited giving leftover food to starving Germans. America and Great Britain placed limits on German industrial and textile production to the extent that the country could not meet the needs of all its citizens and rebuild its economy. Germany paid for the occupation in the form of an Allied tax on goods and services. Many German cities, Payne writes, seethed with anger toward the Americans.

Commentary magazine, in September 1949, published an article titled, "Why Democracy Is Losing in Germany."

Payne notes that the United States did help Germany recover and rebuild by repairing its energy, industrial, water, and health infrastructures. The central question Payne asks, though, is: Would Germany and Europe have recovered on their own without the Marshall Plan? He believes they would have recovered through their own efforts and knowledge. Modern nation-building, he argues, validates his point. Massive foreign aid and intervention by outside forces of nation-builders often push devastated states into further chaos, violence, and tension.

The authors of the viewpoints in this chapter continue Payne's argument whether nation-building can be justified based on accepted notions of history, theory, and intervention.

> "While democracy may not be possible through simply invading and making pronouncements, it may be possible to unleash new ordering forces via temporary social disruption and institutional transplantation."

Transplanting Democratic Institutions Justifies Nation-Building

Max Borders

Max Borders argues in this viewpoint that local, indigenous knowledge in nation-building, the process of so-called spontaneous order, is overrated because nation-building can only be justified by successfully transplanting democratic institutions into new soil. He uses the metaphor of gene splicing, transplanting a new message into a foreign body to regenerate it, as a metaphor for the reviving of the Iraqi people from despotism. Max Borders is the managing editor of TCS Daily *and adjunct scholar with the National Center for Policy Analysis.*

As you read, consider the following questions:

1. According to Borders, what do democratic (positive orders) and failed states (negative orders) have in common?

2. What makes transplantation of state institutions possible, according to the viewpoint author?

3. Borders believes that democratic knowledge in Iraq is converging with what?

With the formation of the new Iraqi government, it's a good time to take stock—not just of the current situation, but of the very idea of nation building.

Many people who read this publication are familiar with the concept known as spontaneous order. The economist Friedrich Hayek pointed out it's the kind of economic and social order that emerges without central planning. Indeed, such order cannot be planned because it is far too complex. The wealth of nations cannot be planned. Neither can nations themselves.

Such ideas underlie one of the primary critiques of "nation-building"—that it is impossible because it requires central planning, which almost always fails. For example, of nation-building, political scientist Gus di Zerega writes: "I think it is criminal, immoral, and hideous. Here I take my Hayekianism [after economist Friedrich Hayek] pretty seriously. Societies cannot be easily molded, the task is too complex, local knowledge is too important."

Negative Spontaneous Orders

But while recognizing the importance of spontaneous order, perhaps it is sometimes forgotten that there are such things as *negative* spontaneous orders. For any organic network of incentives and interests that arises from agents interacting in complex ways, there may be an evil twin. Although power in illiberal states is often largely consolidated and centralized, organic networks of incentives and interests are still the rule here, too—except these networks are maintained by a complex system of patronage, payoffs, theft and fear.

Negative spontaneous orders are today found all over the world, particularly in Africa, Central Asia and the Middle East. And these have a way of sticking around, particularly in the humus soil of foreign aid. Dangerous or failed states, with their legions of poor, emerge like an ergot in the garden of human possibility.

Whatever we think about nation building, we should all be able to agree that both *positive* and *negative* spontaneous orders can and do emerge. A key question becomes: from *what* do they emerge? Institutions, where institutions are, roughly speaking, the internal rule-sets by which a country operates. And there are good institutions and bad institutions.

So—like cancers—dangerous, corrupt, poor, inhumane, confiscatory, and even homicidal states occupy a great swath of the world. The reason for the persistence of negative spontaneous orders is that endogenous [arising from within] institutional change, such as revolution, is both difficult and rare. In addition they persist because spontaneous orders—positive and negative—follow their own logic.

Neither type of order has a *telos* or end, but each has an interest, metaphorically speaking, in its own furtherance, its own survival. Orders, as organisms in their own right, don't care about rights, democracy, prosperity or liberty. Like the processes of evolution, the order's logic is blind, largely internal, and indifferent to the temporal wishes of human actors. That's because deeply entrenched incentive-structures keep any order in place, and in the negative cases, allow predatory leaders and their cronies to suppress dissent and protect their interests—interests that extend through an entire system of venality. And this is in large measure why we should be concerned about negative spontaneous orders wherever they fester.

The Growth of Dangerous Regimes

Many critics of nation-building exercises are virtually silent on the question of what to do about negative orders, except to say "let them alone." After all, as [6th U.S. president] John Quincy Adams admonished: "[America] goes not abroad, in search of monsters to destroy. She is the well-wisher to the freedom and independence of all. She is the champion and vindicator only of her own."

There may be a kernel of truth in Adams's remark. But it has been distorted by critics of nation-building so as to downplay the global interconnections that hold the potential to turn monsters abroad into monsters at home.

If we accept that negative orders follow their own brutal logic of self-perpetuation, we are left with the difficult, rather imperfect job of determining whether those negative orders threaten our own extended order. This is no easy task. But, as globalization pulls both possibilities and problems to our shores, they are very much ours to reckon with.

Neoconservative thinkers have long urged that we should be concerned with the "moral fabric" of various regimes. What they may clumsily or vaguely have been pointing to are the orders that extend from bad institutions, formal and informal. Failed states and dangerous regimes, while they may not be prosperous and free, often still have a growth trajectory. Such growth will have ramifications for our extended order, whether we want to admit it or not. So while neoconservative concern for the moral makeup of dangerous and failed states may strike the Hayekian ear as somewhat dissonant, we have good reason to listen to their intonations.

Can Institutions Be Transplanted?

So what is to be done?

Here's where global strategist and author Thomas P.M. Barnett says it best: we don't have time to sit around and let failed states fester. The United States, for better or worse, is in a position to reverse negative spontaneous orderings through the application of military and other forces. We have a "Leviathan" force that is unequaled on the earth. And we have a deep knowledge of the vital institutions that foster peace and prosperity.

Where I disagree with Barnett is on the question of what comes after a regime change. In a recent article about his book, I emphasized institution-building over nation-building. Barnett responded by saying institution- and nation-building are merely a difference of degree, not of kind, asking: "what is a nation but a collection of institutions?" His response suggests I failed to give enough definition to my intended sense of institutions. Barnett challenged me to tackle the "'how' answers, not just the 'how not' summaries of past experience." And he's right. It's critical not just to clarify what institutions are, but to determine whether or not they can be transplanted.

On the point of clarification, formal institutions are socioeconomic arrangements that bring down the costs of transacting, cooperating, and exchanging. These institutions enable people to interact more freely for mutual benefit and mutual gain, are necessary for prosperity, and ensure checks on the growth of both government and interest groups. Examples are: property rights, individual rights, separation of powers, third-party dispute resolution, suffrage, the common law, contract enforcement, finance/banking, and security.

Why Nation-Building Doesn't Work

Enthusiasts of economic history can go back through the literature and see which societies flourished and which did not according to the de facto rule-sets of a relevant era. Most of the time, institutions evolved through time. In some instances, however, they have been transplanted.

While Barnett comes from the "send in the technocrats" side of the debate, TCS Daily's Arnold Kling comes from the "don't send in anybody" side. Kling recently wrote: "But [...] institutions are not pre-requisites for modernization. They are *results*."

Kling then encouraged those engaged in the debates over institutions and nation-building to engage the arguments he fleshed out in an article titled "Group Power." The crux of Kling's position in "Group Power" is that institutions themselves are the result of endogenous evolution, not exogenous [outside] force. Thus, institution-building in Iraq won't work. What comes out of this and similar points is a general critique of nation-building based on the theoretical inability to create democracy by force and fiat.

But does this critique get it exactly right?

When Building Nations Does Work

Consider this passage about Hong Kong by the Cato Institute's James Dorn:

> Hong Kong's institutions—its set of formal and informal rules—ultimately are shaped by the ethos of society. Hong Kong's ethos of liberty has created a dynamic spontaneous order. Free trade and limited government have provided the opportunities for millions of individuals to use their natural talents to produce a better life for themselves and their families.

Now, here's the paradox: our admiration of Hong Kong must terminate in our admiration of an empire. Without Britannia [the British empire, lasting from the 15th century until the 20th]—with it's free-trade policies and its Common Law legal institutions—Hong Kong might have remained a rather desolate rock. The "ethos" to which Dorn refers coevolved with institutions after a sudden rule-change. In other words, it took the forceful British territorial annexation of Hong Kong after the First Opium War in the mid-1800s to create a major center of commercial activity by 1900, and one of the world's most prosperous cities by 1997, when it was returned to the Chinese. Institutions are shaped by the ethos, yes—but the reverse is also true.

A Dual-Use Reconstruction Force

We should have a military capability that is specifically designed for post-conflict missions. This should be a "dual-use force," because if you actually sit down and do a laundry list of the kind of things you expect the military and its inter-agency partners to do in Baghdad after battle—and you did a laundry list of the kind of things you expected them to do in New Orleans after the flood—the lists are very, very similar. If we built the right kind of force structures in the National Guard, we would have a dual-use force that would have application both in many homeland security settings at home and in many, many operations overseas—in theatre support and post-conflict support, as well as humanitarian operations.

Now specifically, to the reconstruction force: What would it look like? My argument is that it would look something like a constabulary force, which is a military force that is designed to be kind of a hybrid of law enforcement and traditional military. It would have expansive contracting capabilities, like the Army Corps of Engineers, and assessment and management capabilities, like the Federal Emergency Management Agency, and imbedded inspector-general capability. If you put all these things in the blender, I think that is essentially the kind of force structure I would look for.

James Jay Carafano,
"Thinking Diferently About Winning the Peace,"
Heritage Foundation lecture, March 10, 2006. www.heritage.org.

Why Transplanting Institutions Is Possible

So history suggests institutional transplantation is possible—albeit very difficult. What is it about institutions that makes transplantation possible?

Institutions are like the DNA [Deoxyribonucleic Acid that holds the genetic code for living organisms] of a society. Healthy DNA, when expressed, serves as the blueprint for a healthy organism. Likewise, healthy institutions, when in place, allow millions of individual actors to engage in cooperative, mutually beneficial behaviors, the stuff of peace and prosperity. But mutant DNA can create cancer cells. [The dictatorial leaders of] Saddam [Hussein's] Iraq, [Robert] Mugabe's Zimbabwe and [Joseph] Stalin's Russia have (or had) mutant institutions. And pathologies can threaten to spread.

What's more, while institutions can and usually do develop or evolve over time—much in the same way that DNA evolved from auto-catalytic [internally accelerated] processes and from simpler amino acids, and these from yet simpler molecules—once genes are understood and isolated, they can be transplanted, or "spliced."

This genetic analogy suggests the presence of a rule-set, and actors in a given situation will find it beneficial to play by a rule-set or not. They are more likely to comply with new rules if there are positive, self-reinforcing incentives to do so (as well as harsh consequences of non-compliance). The more Iraqis come to understand the incentives generated by positive rule-sets, the more likely positive orders will emerge. But this may require a period of adjustment.

The Iraq Experiment

Iraq, then, may not turn out as we hope. If what the US military and its postwar reconstruction partners hope to achieve is institutional transplantation, then we will have to expect that, sometimes, a host will reject the transplant. With a respectful nod to Arnold Kling's view, informal institutions (culture, religion, beliefs, mores, etc.) may not be at a stage in which the populace is ready to accept a new system of formal rules.

In the case of Iraq, however, it appears the vast majority of citizens are ready to embrace their new institutions. One need only look at the successful democratic elections and public opinion polls of Iraqis to see they are ready for change. (Only a small minority of terrorists and disaffected Ba'athists [Saddam Hussein's political party] is making it difficult and they will have to be captured, killed or reabsorbed via positive incentives.)

This transplantation effort requires both patience and vigilance as we wait for the right kinds of orders to emerge from societal DNA sufficient for a healthy society. If Iraq is conceived as a pity party that requires more resources, more shiny new schools and more dependency, the effort will fail and its new leaders will be corrupted. But if Iraq focuses on incorporating simple systems like security, titled property, and dispute resolution, among others, then they may yet have the ingredients for success.

Nevertheless, a postwar reconstruction effort need not involve massive infusions of resources, manpower, or technical assistance—particularly if these will make the country dependent. Instead, institutional transplantation requires finding those positive incentive structures that allow for the alignment of interests and a commitment to security. By and large, this is what the US seems to be going after in Iraq.

Accelerating Adaptation to Transplantation

On the questions of nation-building, we must look for answers in both theory and practice. In practice, it looks like the Iraq adventure has, if nothing else, shaken up the status quo. Of course, the status quo for Iraq was changed abruptly at the hands of a powerful force. Now it looks like a proto-democracy has taken form, and the Iraqi people seem keen to enter into the modern world. But ripple-effects for the wider Middle East are noticeable, as well. So while democracy may not be possible through simply invading and making pronouncements, it may be possible to unleash new ordering forces via temporary social disruption and institutional transplantation.

The degree to which the shakeup brings an adjustment period of chaos and disunity may actually relate directly to the speed with which a population can adapt to the new rules, as well as the speed with which the people's sentiments (Dorn's "ethos") align with the adaptation. In the case of Iraq, the understanding of democracy and freedom is starting to converge with the process of adapting to the new institutions. On the timescale of history, this has happened pretty quickly.

Success or failure in Iraq cannot be predicted by a priori theories of evolved institutions and spontaneous order alone. Rather, we must learn from our mistakes, tally up our gains, and maintain a level of cautious optimism in the face of a protracted struggle for real institutional change in the region. The rest depends on the mysterious forces deep in the hearts of Iraqis, a place unreachable by pundits of any stripe.

| "Nation building is a lot more compli-
cated and difficult than nation builders
profess to believe."

Transplanting Democratic Institutions Does Not Justify Nation-Building

Alan W. Bock

Alan W. Bock argues in this viewpoint that foreign policy specialists applied their untested notions of nation-building during the Clinton administration based on campaigns against global poverty and promoting global democracy—all with disastrous results. The administration believed they could import democratic institutions to other countries and dispensed with the long-held, and globally recognized, notion of state sovereignty. This opened the door for the dubious nation-building of President George W. Bush. Alan W. Bock is a columnist for the Orange County Register and author of Waiting to Inhale: The Politics of Medical Marijuana.

As you read, consider the following questions:

1. According to Bock, the idea of nation-building comes from where?

Alan W. Bock, "The Folly of Nation Building," *Liberty* magazine, vol. 16, May 2002. http://libertyunbound.com. Copyright © 2002 Liberty Foundation. Reproduced by permission.

2. After the end of the Cold War, foreign policy analysts thought the primary focus of American foreign policy should be what, according to the author?

3. Former U.S. Secretary of State Warren Christopher, during the Clinton administration, stated that the U.S. role in Somalia should be what, according to the viewpoint?

When the war against Afghanistan—or the bombing campaign, depending on how much of a stickler you are for constitutional niceties like declarations of war—was just beginning, I distinctly remember hearing President [George W.] Bush promise quite specifically that the United States wasn't going to get involved in "nation building" in Afghanistan. No, no, we had learned our lessons from the [President Bill] Clinton era. War on evil, yes. Nation building, no.

Bush may have been sincere about this, though no one ever lost any money betting against the sincerity of an American president. But when the slaughter of Asians cooled off, the earlier promise became, as politicians like to say, inoperative. The international dynamics—not to mention the nature of the people who populate the state and defense departments—virtually guaranteed it.

"Fool's Errands," by Gary T. Dempsey and Roger W. Fontaine, could serve as something of a corrective. Most Americans have a vague feeling that the "nation building" adventures in which the Clinton administration dabbled distractedly—Haiti, Somalia, Bosnia, Kosovo—didn't turn out too well, but few believe they were catastrophic. Americans try hard to do the right thing, but those foreigners are just so, well, foreign. Anyway, hardly any Americans came home in body bags.

Not a New Concept

"Fool's Errands" makes it clear that even without the body bags, these ventures caused significant damage to the countries that endured them and to long-run American interests, at least if those interests include minimizing the number of people who resent the United States. They were guided not so much by naive American idealism as by the ideology of nation building, which is more European—or transnational—than American, and ultimately much more naive than simple boosterism. Dempsey and Fontaine tell just how miserably all these missions failed, despite—or perhaps because of—the best exertions of the "best and the brightest."

The notion that the United States is the wielder of virtuous power isn't an entirely new concept. At least since [American president] Woodrow Wilson a certain breed of American internationalist has been entranced with the idea of using power to do good, and a substantial number of internationalists have long been impatient with the idea of national sovereignty. It became more practical to abandon the idea of sovereignty openly, and make "human rights" and "democratic enlargement" the guiding principles once the Soviet Union ceased to be a threat.

The idea of nation building has been floating about for some time in the rarefied atmospheres of academic and diplomatic conferences held in warm-weather vacation spots. But nation building is a lot more complicated and difficult than nation builders profess to believe. In excruciating detail, Dempsey and Fontaine tell just how miserably all these missions failed, despite—or perhaps because of—the best efforts of America's policy elite. It makes for instructive, if hardly inspiring, reading.

The Faith and Failure in Nation-Building

The Clinton administration's "best and brightest" actually seemed to think, for example, that installing [Jean Bertrand] Aristide by force [in 1994] would transform Haiti into a democratic utopia. They got involved in Somalian domestic disputes and squabbles [from 1993-1995] from a position of almost complete and arrogant ignorance, relying on the belief

Kurdistan Versus Iraq

I knew every Kurdish leader that [U.S. Secretary of State Condoleezza] Rice had met with, and I knew not one wanted a unified Iraq. It was not as if the ground truth in Kurdistan [northern Iraq] was hard to discover. Even a casual visitor to Erbil, Kurdistan's capital, notices the Kurdistan flag that flies everywhere, and that the Iraqi flag does not fly at all. (It is banned.) Crossing from Turkey into Kurdistan, the visitor's papers are processed by officials of the Kurdistan Regional Government, and the Iraqi visa requirement does not apply. Kurdistan has its own army and does not allow the new Iraqi Army on its territory. Nor do the Kurds hide their views of Iraq. They hate the country and are not shy about saying so. Understanding this does not require sophisticated analysis. All Rice needed to do was imagine how an American would feel about a country that had gassed you, destroyed your home, and executed hundreds of thousands of your kinsmen—and which you never wanted to be a part of in the first place.

Peter W. Galbraith, The End of Iraq, *2006, p. 99.*

that military force and good intentions would ineluctably solve tribal rivalries that have gone on for centuries. They created a "multiethnic" Bosnia and tried to manipulate its domestic politics when it proved unstable. They openly played favorites in Bosnia and Kosovo [intervening in 1996], creating widespread resentment against the United States from all sides.

Most of these failures have been reported by the American press. Dempsey and Fontaine stitch the loose threads into a larger tapestry of failure. And they explain the kind of thinking that leads to failure.

These Clinton-era fiascoes, the authors conclude, "were expressions of the administration's faith in the power of government, especially the U.S. government, to engineer solutions to political and social problems." At the end of the administration, with failure after failure staring him in the face, Clinton said, "We've got to realize that there are other places in the world that we haven't fooled with enough." The White House then presented a "new development agenda for the 21st century" with an "accelerated campaign against global poverty" and the elimination of the "digital divide," and advocated "democratic enlargement" as a uniquely American (i.e., bureaucratic) response to globalism. Clinton's people were quite open and explicit about the fact that their program meant an end to outdated concepts like national sovereignty and that it would cost a great deal in military force and foreign aid.

Abandoning Equal Sovereignty

"Fool's Errands" provides extensive quotations from academic proponents of nation building, many of whom had the chance to apply their theories as officials during the Clinton administration. They explicitly abandon the theory of equal sovereignty among nations, which has been a governing principle of international law for almost a century—and which was designed to minimize international conflict. The principle of equal sovereignty holds that what a sovereign state does inside its borders is its own business, even if it is reprehensible to others. Military action is justified only when a country takes action outside its borders, by making war on or interfering in the internal affairs of another sovereign state.

Although the principle of equal sovereignty was sometimes exploited by repressive regimes (e.g., the Soviets and Chinese) and, like any general rule of action, had gray areas— (when a subsidy to a foreign opposition group becomes an interference that could be called aggressive, for example)—most states respected the sovereignty of other states.

A Futile Promotion of Democracy

With the end of the Cold War [fight for global dominance between the United States and the Soviet Union, 1945–1991], however, came much chin-rubbing about the proper role of the United States in a world in which it was no longer needed to contain the Soviet Union. As Dempsey and Fontaine put it, "One theme that proved popular with the foreign policy establishment—and which coincidentally required maintaining Cold War-era levels of global activism and defense spending—was 'promoting democracy.'"

Scholars left and right, including Morton Halperin, Tufts professor Tony Smith, Harvard professor Stanley Hoffman, and American Enterprise [a conservative think-tank organization] fellows Joshua Muravchik and Michael Ledeen, wrote articles and books arguing that the primary goal of American foreign policy should be to "promote democracy." [Former Clinton administration] National security adviser Anthony Lake noted in a 1993 speech that the United States had successfully contained threats to market democracies, but "now we should seek to enlarge their reach. We should strengthen the community of major market democracies. We need to pursue our humanitarian agenda not only by providing aid but also by working to help democracy and market economies take root in regions of greatest humanitarian concern." This became policy when [former Clinton administration] Secretary of State Warren Christopher announced in June, 1993, that the Clinton administration's goal in Somalia was not simply to contain a potential threat, but to play "a sturdy American role to help the United Nations rebuild a viable nation-state." Although the term "nation building" was abandoned after the Somalia debacle, the same motive prompted U.S. interventions in Haiti, Bosnia, and Kosovo.

By the end of the 1990s, the pretense of respecting national sovereignty had virtually disappeared. There were crusades to wage. Bill Clinton told [CNN corespondent] Wolf

Blitzer in June, 1999, shortly after the end of the NATO bombing campaign in Kosovo: "Whether within or beyond the borders of a country, if the world community has the power to stop it, we ought to stop genocide and ethnic cleansing." This echoed what then-U.N. Secretary General Javier Perez de Cuellar had said as long ago as 1991, "that the defense of the oppressed in the name of morality should prevail over frontiers and legal documents." [Former Sudanese diplomat and UN Secretary General's representative for refugees] Francis Deng declared that the concept of sovereignty should be "reinterpreted as a concept of responsibility to protect one's own citizens. The sovereign has to become responsible or forfeit sovereignty." Jan Vederveen of the Institute for Social Studies in the Netherlands averred that "It is not so much that sovereignty is becoming an 'archaic' notion, as some assert, but that it is increasingly being viewed as conditional in relation to human rights."

Human Rights Crusades Become Aggression

I am tempted to give two cheers for the notion that human rights are more important than state sovereignty. But in practice this notion has been used mainly to justify intervention and aggression (what else would you call a bombing campaign?) by the biggest, most powerful state in the world, or by an agglomeration of powerful countries.

Perhaps it would do no good to send copies of "Fool's Errands" to members of Congress and to executive-branch policymakers. But if you're uneasy about the notion of nation building, this book will give you even more powerful reasons to be concerned.

> *"If the international community is un-
> willing to allow states to be rebuilt by
> wars, it must provide the military
> muscle in the form of a sufficiently
> strong peacekeeping force. Like it or not,
> military might is a necessary compo-
> nent of state building."*

Nation-Building in Failed States Is Justified

Marina Ottoway

*Marina Ottoway is a senior associate at the Carnegie Endow-
ment for International Peace and codirector of its Democracy
and Rule of Law Project. Nation-building has a long history, Ottoway states in this viewpoint, but that perspective should not
make us naive about its use today. Ottoway argues that ad hoc
and failed states will require nation-building or risk becoming
security threats to the world. The goal of nation-building is not
always fostering democracy, she argues, and unpleasant compromises will have to be made, to stabilize drastic state failures like
Afghanistan.*

Marina Ottoway, "Nation Building (Think Again)," *Foreign Policy*, September-October
2002. Copyright © 2002 by Carnegie Endowment for International Peace. Reproduced
by permission.

As you read, consider the following questions:

1. According to Ottoway, what are the three types of nation-building with the most lasting impact on the world?

2. What are quasi-states, as defined by Ottoway?

3. When do nongovernmental organizations (NGOs) cause the most problems in nation-building, according to Ottoway?

4. The international political will to save failed states exists, according to Ottoway. What is the largest stumbling block to rebuilding all failed states that she defines in the viewpoint?

Take a look at how the political map of the world has changed in every century since the collapse of the Roman Empire—that should be proof enough that nation building has been around for quite a while. Casting a glance at the 19th and 20th centuries will reveal that the types of nation building with the most lasting impact on the modern world are nationalism, colonialism, and post-World War II reconstruction.

Nationalism gave rise to most European countries that exist today. The theory was that each nation, embodying a shared community of culture and blood, was entitled to its own state. (In reality, though, few beyond the intellectual and political elite shared a common identity.) This brand of nationalism led to the reunification of Italy in 1861 and Germany in 1871 and to the breakup of Austria-Hungary in 1918. This process of nation building was successful where governments were relatively capable, where powerful states decided to make room for new entrants, and where the population of new states was not deeply divided. Germany had a capable government and succeeded so well in forging a common identity that the entire world eventually paid for it. Yugoslavia, by contrast, failed in its efforts, and the international community is still sorting out the mess.

Nations Built by War

Colonial powers formed dozens of new states as they conquered vast swaths of territory, tinkered with old political and leadership structures, and eventually replaced them with new countries and governments. Most of today's collapsed states, such as Somalia or Afghanistan, are a product of colonial nation building. The greater the difference between the precolonial political entities and what the colonial powers tried to impose, the higher the rate of failure.

The transformation of West Germany and Japan into democratic states following World War II is the most successful nation-building exercise ever undertaken from the outside. Unfortunately, this process took place under circumstances unlikely to be repeated elsewhere. Although defeated and destroyed, these countries had strong state traditions and competent government personnel. West Germany and Japan were nation-states in the literal sense of the term—they were ethnic and cultural communities as well as political states. And they were occupied by the U.S. military, a situation that precluded choices other than the democratic state. . . .

The most successful nations, including the United States and the countries of Europe, were built by war. These countries achieved statehood because they developed the administrative capacity to mobilize resources and to extract the revenue they needed to fight wars.

State Building Through Coercion

Some countries have been created not by their own efforts but by decisions made by the international community. The Balkans [southeast region of Europe, including Bosnia, Croatia, and Serbia] offer unfortunate examples of states cobbled together from pieces of defunct empires. Many African countries exist because colonial powers chose to grant them independence. The British Empire created most modern states in the Middle East by carving up the territory of the defeated Ottoman Empire. The Palestinian state, if it becomes a reality, will be another example of a state that owes its existence to an international decision.

Such countries have been called quasi-states—entities that exist legally because they are recognized internationally but that hardly function as states in practice because they do not have governments capable of controlling their territory. Some quasi-states succeed in retrofitting a functioning country into the legalistic shell. The state of Israel, for example, was formed because of an international decision, and Israel immediately demonstrated its staying power by waging a successful war to defend its existence. But many quasi-states fail and then become collapsed states.

Today, war is not an acceptable means of state building. Instead, nation building must be a consensual, democratic process. But such a process is not effective against adversaries who are not democratic, who have weapons, and who are determined to use them. The world should not be fooled into thinking that it is possible to build states without coercion. If the international community is unwilling to allow states to be rebuilt by wars, it must provide the military muscle in the form of a sufficiently strong peacekeeping force. Like it or not, military might is a necessary component of state building. . . .

Security by Military Might

[Former] White House National Security Advisor Condoleezza Rice [who became the U.S. secretary of state in 2005] had a point when she quipped during the 2000 presidential campaign that the [8]2nd Airborne has more important task than "escorting kids to kindergarten." But no one ever said that the primary task of U.S. troops should be babysitting. If the inter-

State-Building Is Messy

History teaches another important lesson: that occupation duty sometimes leads troops to commit what are today called human rights abuses. It is easy to exaggerate the extent of these excesses. Brian Linn's recent history, *The Philippine War 1899–1902*, suggests that the conduct of American soldiers from 1899 to 1902 was not nearly as reprehensible as everyone from Mark Twain to New Left historians of the 1960s would have us believe.

But whenever a small number of occupation troops are placed in the midst of millions of potentially hostile foreigners, some unpleasant episodes are likely to occur. During the U.S. occupation of the Dominican Republic from 1916 to 1924, a marine captain named Charles F. Merkel became notorious as the Tiger of Seibo; he personally tortured one prisoner by slashing him with a knife, pouring salt and orange juice into the wounds, and then cutting off the man's ears. Merkel killed himself in jail after, rumor had it, a visit from two marine officers who left him a gun with a single bullet in it. When word of such abuses reached the United States, it caused a public uproar. In the 1920 election the Republican presidential candidate, Warren G. Harding, sought black votes by denouncing the "rape" of Hispaniola perpetrated by a Democratic administration. This kind of criticism is not so different from the questions raised today about [U.S.] treatment of Taliban or Iraqi prisoners.

Max Boot, "Neither New nor Nefarious: The Liberal Empire Strikes Back," Current History, *November 2003.*

national community does not want to give war a chance by allowing adversaries to fight until someone prevails, then it has to establish control through a military presence willing to use deadly force. And if nation building is in the interests of the United States (as the [President George W.] Bush administration has reluctantly concluded), then the United States must participate in imposing that control.

It is not enough just to participate in the initial effort (in the war fought from the sky), because what counts is what happens on the ground afterward. Newly formed states need long-term plans that go beyond the recent mission statement outlined by one U.S. diplomat: "We go in, we hunt down terrorists, and we go out as if we'd never been there." Even if the United States succeeds in eliminating the last pockets of the Taliban [fundamentalist Islamic group that ruled Afghanistan from 1996 to 2001] and al Qaeda in Afghanistan, Americans could face another threat in a few years. And although warring armies are no longer active in Bosnia, the country would splinter apart if international troops went home.

The United States does not have to take the central role in peacekeeping operations, but U.S. participation is important because the country is the most powerful member of the international community. Otherwise, the United States sends the message that it doesn't care what happens next—and in doing so, it undermines fragile new governments and encourages the emergence of feuding factions and warlords. . . .

A Lack of Political Will

Many of the nation-building methods used in the past are inconceivable today, but the international community has yet to find effective substitutes. For instance, the first step colonial powers took when engaging in nation building was "pacification," invariably a bloody undertaking described by the British writer Rudyard Kipling as "the savage wars of peace." In today's gentler world of nation building, such violent means are fortunately unacceptable. Instead, peacemakers usually try to mediate agreements among rival factions, demobilize combatants, and then reintegrate them in civilian life—a theoretically good idea that rarely works in practice.

Political will for state reconstruction is also in short supply nowadays. That's hardly surprising, given that countries expected to help rebuild nations are the same ones that until recently were accused of neoimperialism. Sierra Leoneans today welcome the British peacekeeping force with open arms and even wax nostalgic about the old days of British rule. But they revolted against British colonialism in the 1950s, and not so long ago, they condemned it as the root cause of all their problems. Should we be surprised that the British are, at best, ambivalent about their role?

And even when the international community demonstrates the will to undertake nation building, it's not always able to figure out who should shoulder the burden. The international community is an unwieldy entity with no single center and lots of contradictions. It comprises the major world powers, with the United States as the dominant agent in some situations and as a reluctant participant in others. In Afghanistan, for instance, the United States wants to have complete control over war operations but refuses to have anything to do with peacekeeping. Meanwhile, the multilateral organization that by its mandate should play the dominant role in peacekeeping and state reconstruction—the United Nations—is the weakest and most divided of all. . . .

The Role and Danger of NGOs

Large international nongovernmental organizations (NGOs), such as Oxfam or CARE, are vital in distributing humanitarian assistance in collapsed states. They go into high-risk, lawless regions where international agencies and bilateral donors are unwilling to operate. But these organizations can also become part of the problem. In Somalia, for instance, protection money paid by international NGOs to gain safe passage for food and medical supplies financed the purchase of weapons by warlords and contributed to the escalation of violence.

To operate effectively, international and national NGOs need the stability that only states can provide. These organizations must also coordinate their activities with states so as not to undermine reconstruction efforts. For example, NGOs can play an essential role in administering healthcare in countries where the government has little outreach, but they can also create havoc if they insist on operating independently of the central government and of each other. That's what happened in Mozambique during the 1980s, when NGOs diverted funds from the public sector and fragmented the national health system.

In Afghanistan right now there is considerable tension between the central government (which has little capacity to deliver humanitarian relief and services but feels that it should coordinate the effort) and international NGOs (which have greater capacity and experience). For the time being, NGOs are the most effective channel for delivering aid, but if government institutions are not allowed to take more long-term responsibility, nation building will fail. . . .

Strategic Variables

"No sane person opposes nation-building in places that count," writes conservative columnist Charles Krauthammer. "The debate is about nation-building in places that don't." But this type of reasoning eventually forced the United States to fight a war in Afghanistan, a country deemed so unimportant after the Soviets departed that it was left to become a battleground for warlords and a safe haven for al Qaeda [alliance of terrorist groups, founded by Osama bin-Laden in 1988]. In 1994, the United States abandoned strategically insignificant Somalia, too, only to start worrying after September 11, 2001 [terrorist attacks], whether that country had also been infiltrated by terrorist networks.

For most countries, strategic significance is a variable, not a constant. Certainly, some countries, such as China, are always significant. But even countries that appear of marginal or no importance can suddenly become crucial. Afghanistan is not the only example. In the days of the Cold War, countries or regions suddenly became prominent when they were befriended by the Soviet Union. "SALT [Strategic Arms Limitation Talks between the U.S. and U.S.S.R.]," then National Security Advisor [to President Jimmy Carter] Zbigniew Brzezinski declared in 1980, "was buried in the sands of the Ogaden [part of the volatile Somalia region within Ethiopa]"—referring to the cooling of U.S.-Soviet relations when the countries were dragged in to support opposite sides in a war between Ethiopia and Somalia. A few years later, the Reagan administration sent people scrambling for small-scale maps of Lebanon by declaring that Souk el-Gharb, an obscure crossroads town, was vital to U.S. security.

The lesson by now should be clear: No country is so insignificant that it can never become important. So, by all means, let us focus our efforts only on strategically important countries, as long as we can predict which ones they are. (Good luck.)

Democratic Cheap

Let us not indulge in fantasy. It is politically correct to equate state reconstruction with democracy building. Indeed, the international community has a one-size-fits-all model for democratic reconstruction, so that plans devised for Afghanistan bear a disturbing resemblance to those designed for the Democratic Republic of the Congo (DRC). This model usually envisages a negotiated settlement to the conflict and the holding of a national conference of major domestic groups (the loya jirga in Afghanistan and the Inter-Congolese Dialogue in the DRC) to reach an agreement on the structure of the political system, followed by elections. In addition to these core activities, the model calls for subsidiary but crucial undertakings, beginning with the demobilization of former combatants and the development of a new national army, then extending to reforming the judiciary, restructuring the civil service, and establishing a central bank—thus creating all the institutions deemed necessary to run a modern state.

This model is enormously expensive, requiring major commitments of money and personnel on the part of the international community. As a result, this approach has only been implemented seriously in the case of Bosnia, the only country where the international community has made an open-ended commitment of money and power to see the job through to the end. Six years [as of 2002] into the process, progress is excruciatingly slow and not even a glimmer of light is waiting at the end of the tunnel. But elsewhere in the world, including Afghanistan, the international community prescribes this model without providing the resources. The most obvious missing resource in Afghanistan is a robust international peacekeeping force.

Unpleasant Choices

The issue here is not simply political will. The resources are just not available. Consider the list of current nation-building projects: Bosnia, Kosovo, Afghanistan, Sierra Leone, the DRC, and Burundi. Plus, Somalia is again on the international radar screen. If an agreement is reached, nation-building efforts will begin in Sudan. . . . Meanwhile, the international community has to cough up the nearly $400 million it pledged to fund the budget of the nascent Afghanistan government.

Consequently, the international community has to set more modest goals for nation building and then tailor those goals to each country's reality. Unpleasant compromises are inevitable. If the international community is not going to disarm Afghanistan's warlords, it will have to deal with them in other ways because they will not just disappear on their own. It has to make at least some of them less dangerous and disruptive by using aid to co-opt them into the government. If nations do not want to occupy Somalia and impose state structures on warring clans, they should consider helping the regional governments that have emerged to fill the void, beginning with Somaliland [self-declared independent republic within Somalia]. In some cases, such as in the DRC, the international community should either accept the disintegration of the country or allow nondemocratic leaders to use force to put the state back together. These are all unpalatable choices. But those who believe that the international community knows how to turn collapsed states into democracies should think again.

"People who believe that failed states pose a threat to U.S. security and that nation building is the answer see the world as both simpler and more threatening than it is."

Nation-Building in Failed States Is Not Justified

Christopher Preble and Justin Logan

Christopher Preble and Justin Logan argue in this viewpoint that the overwhelming majority of failed states pose no serious security threat to the United States. Nation-building in failed states is extraordinarily expensive when compared to the return on investment. The authors argue there is no good model, fiscal or military, for nation-building. Christopher Preble is director of foreign policy studies at the Cato Institute. Justin Logan is foreign policy analyst at the institute.

As you read, consider the following questions:

1. The authors argue in the viewpoint that failed states are not the product of state collapse itself. What are the other factors that cause state failure?

Christopher Preble and Justin Logan, "Are Failed States a Threat to America?" *Reason* magazine, July 1, 2006. Copyright 2006 by Reason Foundation, 3415 S. Sepulveda Blvd., Suite 400, Los Angeles, CA 90034. www.reason.com. Reproduced by permission.

2. How does the U.S. Defense Science Board calculate the requirements of saving a failed state, according to the viewpoint?

3. Do the authors believe that, if the United States refuses nation-building in failed states, it will lead to a world collapse?

The idea that state failure is inherently threatening to the United States has been circulating for some time. In an influential 1994 article, *The Atlantic Monthly*'s Robert Kaplan sounded the alarm about "the coming anarchy," urging Western strategists to start worrying about "what is occurring . . . throughout West Africa and much of the underdeveloped world: the withering away of central governments, the rise of tribal and regional domains, the unchecked spread of disease, and the growing pervasiveness of war." He warned that "the coming upheaval, in which foreign embassies are shut down, states collapse, and contact with the outside world takes place through dangerous, disease-ridden coastal trading posts, will loom large in the century we are entering." He argued that insecurity and instability in remote regions should be high on the list of post-Cold War [after 1991] foreign policy concerns because the damage and depredations of the Third World would not always be contained, and would inevitably—though he doesn't really explain how—touch the lives of those in America and Western Europe. Although humanitarianism was the most frequently heard justification for the Clinton administration's attempts at nation building, the president's defenders in and out of government also offered a Kaplanesque rationale that fixing failed states would make the U.S. safer.

Despite his initial skepticism toward Clinton-era nation building, President [George W.] Bush changed course dramatically after September 11, 2001. The *United States National Security Strategy*, released in September 2002, made "expand-[ing] the circle of development by opening societies and building the infrastructure of democracy" a central plank of

America's response to the 9/11 attacks. Part of the administration's new security policy would be to "help build police forces, court systems, and legal codes, local and provincial government institutions, and electoral systems." The overarching goal was to "make the world not just safer but better."

Making the World Safe Through Democracy

According to the administration's October 2005 *National Intelligence Strategy*, "the lack of freedom in one state endangers the peace and freedom of others, and . . . failed states are a refuge and breeding ground of extremism." The strategy therefore asks our overworked intelligence services not just to gather information on America's enemies but to "bolster the growth of democracy and sustain peaceful democratic states." The premise is, as the former Cato foreign policy analyst Gary Dempsey put it, that "if only we could populate the planet with 'good' states, we could eradicate international conflict and terrorism."

Many foreign policy pundits agree with the Bush administration's goal of making the world safe through democracy. Lawrence J. Korb and Robert O. Boorstin of the Center for American Progress, for example, warn in a 2005 report that "weak and failing states pose as great a danger to the American people and international stability as do potential conflicts among the great powers." A 2003 report from the Center for Strategic and International Studies agrees that "as a superpower with a global presence and global interests, the United States does have a stake in remedying failed states." In the course of commenting on a report from the Center for Global Development, Francis Fukuyama, a professor at the Johns Hopkins School of Advanced International Studies, argued that "it should be abundantly clear that state weakness and failure [are] the single most critical threat to U.S. national security."

Even foreign policy specialists known for their hard-nosed realism have succumbed to the idea that nation building is a matter of self-defense. A 2005 Council on Foreign Relations task force co-chaired by Brent Scowcroft, national security adviser in the first Bush administration and a critic of the current war in Iraq, produced a report that insists "action to stabilize and rebuild states marked by conflict is not 'foreign policy as social work,' a favorite quip of the 1990s. It is equally a humanitarian concern and a national security priority." The report says stability operations should be "a strategic priority for the armed forces" and the national security adviser should produce an "overarching policy associated with stabilization and reconstruction activities."

State Failure Does Not Equal a Threat

Those arguments suffer not so much from inaccuracy as from analytical sloppiness. It would be absurd to claim that the ongoing state failure in Haiti poses a national security threat of the same order as would state failure in Indonesia, with its population of 240 million, or in nuclear-armed Pakistan. In fact, the overwhelming majority of failed states have posed no security threat to the United States. Take, for example, the list of countries identified as failed or failing by *Foreign Policy* magazine and the Fund for Peace in 2005. Using 12 different indicators of state failure, the researchers derived state failure scores, and then listed 60 countries whose cumulative scores marked them as "critical," "in danger," or "borderline," ranked in order. If state failure is itself threatening, then we should get very concerned about the Democratic Republic of the Congo, Sierra Leone, Chad, Bangladesh, and on and on.

In short, state failure ranks rather low as an accurate metric for measuring threats. Likewise, while the lists of "failed states" and "security threats" will no doubt overlap, correlation does not equal causation. The obvious nonthreats that appear

Are These Failed States a Threat?

The Failed States Index Rankings			Indicators of Instability			
Rank	Total	County	Refugees and Displaced Persons	Economy	Human Rights	External Intervention
1	112.3	Sudan	9.7	7.5	9.8	9.8
2	110.1	Dem. Rep. of the Congo	9.5	8.1	9.5	10.0
3	109.2	Ivory Coast	7.6	9.0	9.4	10.0
4	109.0	Iraq	8.3	8.2	9.7	10.0
5	108.9	Zimbabwe	8.9	9.8	9.5	8.0
6	105.9	Chad	9.0	7.9	9.1	8.0
7	105.9	Somalia	8.1	8.5	9.5	8.5
8	104.6	Haiti	5.0	8.4	9.6	10.0
9	103.1	Pakistan	9.3	7.0	8.5	9.2
10	99.8	Afghanistan	9.6	7.5	8.2	10.0

TAKEN FROM: Foreign Policy and Fund for Peace, "Failed States Index, 2006," www.foreignpolicy.com.

on all lists of failed states undermine the claim that there is something particular about failed states that is necessarily threatening.

The dangers that can arise from failed states are not the product of state failure itself. They are the result of other factors, such as the presence of terrorist cells or other malign actors. Afghanistan in the late 1990s met anyone's definition of a failed state, and the chaos in Afghanistan clearly contributed to [Al Qaeda leader] Osama bin Laden's decision to relocate his operations there from Sudan in 1996. But the security threat to America arose from cooperation between Al Qaeda and the Taliban government, which tolerated the organization's training camps. Afghanistan under the Taliban was both a failed state and a threat, but in that respect it was a rarity. More common are failed states, from the Ivory Coast to Burma, that pose no threat to us at all.

It's true that Al Qaeda and other terrorist organizations can operate in failed states. But they also can (and do) operate in Germany, Canada, and other countries that are not failed states by any stretch of the imagination. Rather than making categorical statements about failed states, we should assess the extent to which any given state or nonstate actors within it intend and have the means to attack America. Afghanistan is a stark reminder that we must not overlook failed states, but it does not justify making them our top security concern.

A Cure Worse than the Disease

If state failure does not in itself pose a threat to U.S. security, an ambitious program of nation building would, in turn, be a cure worse than the disease. One particularly troubling prospect is the erosion of internationally recognized sovereignty. As Winston Churchill said of democracy, sovereignty may be the worst system around, except for all the others. A system of sovereignty grants a kernel of legitimacy to regimes that rule barbarically; it values as equals countries that clearly are not;

and it frequently enforces borders that were capriciously drawn by imperial powers. But it's far from clear that any available alternative is better.

Yet in his previous life as an academic, Stephen Krasner, [named] director of policy planning at the U.S. State Department [in 2005], flatly declared that the "rules of conventional sovereignty no longer work." A stroll through the work of scholars who support nation building reveals such alternative concepts as "shared sovereignty," "trusteeships," even "postmodern imperialism." (The latter is supposed to mean an attempt to manipulate domestic politics in foreign countries without all that old-fashioned imperial messiness.)

If the United States proceeds on a course of nation building, based largely on the premise that sovereignty should be de-emphasized, where will that logic stop? Who gets to decide which states retain their sovereignty and which states forfeit it? Will other powers use our own rhetoric against us to justify expansionist foreign policies? It's not hard to envision potential flashpoints in eastern Europe and East Asia.

An American exceptionalist might reply that the *United States* gets to decide, because we're different. But such an argument is unlikely to prevent other countries from using our own logic against us. If we tug at the thread of sovereignty, the whole sweater may quickly unravel.

Chances for Success Are Slim

An aggressive nation-building strategy would also detract from the struggle against terrorism, by diverting attention and resources, puncturing the mystique of American power, and provoking anger through promiscuous foreign intervention. A prerequisite for nation building is establishing security in the target country, which requires the presence of foreign troops, something that often inspires terrorism. In a survey of suicide terrorism between 1980 and 2003, University of Chicago political scientist Robert A. Pape concluded that almost all suicide attacks "have in common . . . a specific secular and strategic goal: to compel modern democracies to withdraw military forces from territory that the terrorists consider to be their homeland."

Such risks might be justified if the chances of success were high. But history suggests they're not. In the most thorough survey of American nation-building missions, the RAND Corporation [organization that analyzes national security issues] in 2003 evaluated seven cases: Japan and West Germany after World War II, Somalia in 1992–94, Haiti in 1994–96, Bosnia from 1995 to the present, Kosovo from 1999 to the present, and Afghanistan from 2001 to the present. Assessing the cases individually, the authors count Japan and West Germany as successes but all the others as failures to various degrees. They then try to determine what made the Japanese and West German operations succeed when all the nation-building efforts since have failed.

Their answer is complex and not entirely satisfying. To the extent that any clear conclusion can be drawn from this research, the report says, it is that "nation building . . . is a time- and resource-consuming effort." Indeed, "among controllable factors, the most important determinant is the level of effort—measured in time, manpower, and money."

In its 2004 *Summer Study on Transition to and From Hostilities*, the Defense Science Board, a panel that advises the Defense Department on strategy, reached a similar conclusion. Although "postconflict success often depends on significant political changes," it said, the "barriers to transformation of [an] opponent's society [are] immense." And in the absence of a decisive outcome between warring parties (such as happened in World War II), there is always a danger that violence will continue.

It Can't Be Built Cheap

Not surprisingly, successful nation building is highly contingent on security within the target country. The non-warfighting roles a nation-building military has to play would be tremendously taxing for both the armed services and the U.S. treasury.

By the Defense Science Board's calculations, achieving "ambitious goals" in a failed state requires 20 foreign soldiers per 1,000 inhabitants. Applying this ratio to a few top-ranked failed states yields sobering results. Nation building in the Ivory Coast would require 345,000 foreign troops. Sudan would take 800,000. Iraq, where the U.S. and its allies have 153,000 troops [as of 2006], would need 520,000. And if history is any guide, effective execution would require deployments of 10 years or longer.

All this means that nation-building missions are extremely expensive, regardless of whether they succeed or fail. Zalmay Khalilzad, former U.S. ambassador to Afghanistan and current ambassador to Iraq, believes that in the case of Afghanistan, "it will take annual assistance [of $4.5 billion] or higher for five to seven years to achieve our goals." Operation Uphold Democracy in Haiti, which restored a government and installed 8,000 peacekeepers but left that country in its perpetual state of chaos, cost more than $2 billion. Operations Provide Relief and Restore Hope in Somalia, which provided tons of food as humanitarian relief (which were in turn looted by warlords) and eventually got dozens of Americans killed and injured, leading to a hasty and disastrous American retreat, ended up costing $2.2 billion. As of 2002 the United States had spent more than $23 billion intervening in the Balkans since the early '90s. In Iraq, we have already crested the $300 billion mark [as of 2006], having decided that the vagaries of Iraqi sectarian politics should decide our future mission in that country.

Even Francis Fukuyama, a staunch advocate of nation building, admits such efforts have "an extremely troubled record of success." As Fukuyama wrote in his 2005 book *State Building: Governance and World Order in the 21st Century*, "It is not simply that nation building hasn't worked; in cases like sub-Saharan Africa, many of these efforts have actually eroded institutional capacity over time." Put simply, there is no "model" for nation building. The few broad lessons we can draw indicate that success depends on a relentless determination to impose a nation's will, manifested in many years of occupation and billions of dollars in spending.

In this light, the position of the more extreme neo-imperialists is more realistic than that of nation builders who think we can fix failed states on the cheap. The Harvard historian Niall Ferguson argues that a proper approach to Iraq would put up to 1 million foreign troops on the ground there for up to 70 years. If resources were unlimited, or if the American people were prepared to shoulder such a burden, that might be a realistic suggestion. But the notion that such enterprises can be carried out quickly and inexpensively is badly mistaken.

Less America Does Not Spell Disaster

People who believe that failed states pose a threat to U.S. security and that nation building is the answer see the world as both simpler and more threatening than it is. Failed states generally do not represent security threats. At the same time, nation building in failed states is very difficult and usually unsuccessful.

There is certainly a point at which Robert Kaplan's "coming anarchy," if it were to materialize, would threaten American interests. Here's how Ferguson, in *Foreign Policy* magazine, describes a world in which America steps back from its role as a global policeman: "Waning empires. Religious revivals. Incipient anarchy. A coming retreat into fortified cities. These are the Dark Age experiences that a world without a hyper-power might quickly find itself reliving."

It's telling that to find a historical precedent on which to base his argument, Ferguson has to reach back to the ninth century. His prediction of a "Dark Age" hinges on a belief that America will collapse (because of excessive consumption, an inadequate army, and an imperial "attention deficit"), the European Union will collapse (because of an inflexible welfare state and shifting demographics), and China will collapse (because of a currency or banking crisis). There is little reason to believe that if America refuses to administer foreign countries, the world will go down this path. The fact that advocates of fixing failed states have to rely on such outlandish scenarios to build their case tells us a good deal about the merit of their arguments.

> "The talent of the Bush Administration
> was not to face the reality of
> Afghanistan's warlordism or merely
> manage it—they had no choice—but
> to embrace it, to use it fully and
> shrewdly as a powerful instrument for
> nation-building."

Nation-Building with Warlords Is Justified

John C. Hulsman and Alexis Y. Debat

*John C. Hulsman and Alexis Y. Debat argue in this viewpoint
that most nation-building is flawed because of its failure to work
with native clan leaders and warlords. Nation-building should
focus on recruiting indigenous warlords who understand the ethnic history of their country. Warlords, the authors argue, would
help rebuilders achieve realistic goals at the clan level. John C.
Hulsman is a senior research fellow at the Heritage Foundation
and coauthor of* Ethical Realism and American Foreign Policy.
*Alexis Y. Debat is a senior fellow at George Washington
University's Homeland Security Policy Institute and a terrorism
consultant to ABC News.*

John C. Hulsman, and Alexis Y. Debat, "In Praise of Warlords," *The National Interest*,
summer 2006, pp. 50-58. www.nationalinterest.org. Copyright © *The National Interest*
2006, Washington, D.C. Reproduced by permission.

As you read, consider the following questions:

1. How do the authors define "warlord"?

2. T.E. Lawrence was successful in working with Arab and Syrian tribes during World War I, according to the viewpoint. How does his work contrast with modern nation-building, according to the authors?

3. What is the moral rule the United States should use when nation-building and working with warlords, according to the authors?

Legitimacy comes in many faces. Westerners like to see it in the glow of freedom fighters ascending to high office in a sweeping democratic process, preferably after mass rallies in the squares of capital cities with the attendant flags and banners and rock concerts. But we are loath to grace with "legitimacy" the evil, greedy chieftain of Western imagination—the warlord—conjured in no small part by the portrayals in Indiana Jones movies. Of course, the West might work with such unsavory characters in alliances of convenience, but they are to be despised (not least in their immoral challenge to Western democratic superiority) and then quickly done away with at the first possible opportunity—to be replaced by "proper" political figures.

Our cinematic reaction to warlords has carried over into the policies of American state-builders to an uncomfortable degree. When looked at in the glare of reality, America's state-building record in the post-Cold War era [after 1991] is dreadful because of our reflexive antipathy for warlords and our unwillingness to co-opt them. America's failure to identify and engage warlords has contributed again and again to the most conspicuous of U.S. nation-building failures.

Flaws in the Western Model

In Haiti we intervened to put a Robespierreist [after one of the leaders of the French Revolution, 1789–1799] president,

Jean-Bertrand Aristide, back in power following a military coup. After he pathetically failed even to begin addressing Haiti's massive problems, cultivated authoritarian tendencies, and failed to draw in the country's factional power brokers, Aristide was again chased into exile, this time in Africa. Haiti remains the poorest country in the Western Hemisphere.

In Bosnia America's failure to grasp the durability of clan and ethnic allegiances undermined peacekeeping efforts. If free and fair elections were held tomorrow, two of the three primary ethnic groups (the Bosnian Serbs and the Bosnian Croats) would vote to secede from the country, a decade after the Dayton Accords.

In Afghanistan things are a little better. President Hamid Karzai, following successes in both the presidential and parliamentary elections, is finally more than just the mayor of Kabul [Afghanistan's capital]. But anyone assuming that in the foreseeable future he will be able to supervise, bypass or pacify the country's powerful warlords—especially now that they are represented in Parliament—needs an Internet connection. And, of course, there is Iraq.

This dismal record is matched by an unwillingness to seriously assess the flaws in the standard Western model of statebuilding from afar. Debates continue to focus on the potential roles of the United States, United Nations, World Bank, European Union or International Monetary Fund [international organization that oversees global financial systems] in statebuilding, with indigenous leadership—chiefs, elders and yes, even warlords—playing either a secondary or adversarial role in the process.

Meet the Warlord

As long as international admiration trumps local legitimacy in selecting who we are willing to work with in state-building, our efforts will fail. This means, in many parts of the world, we have to come to terms with so-called warlords.

But just what do we mean by "warlord"? A "warlord" is a leader whose power has been attained by non-democratic means but who exercises authority usually on the basis of an appeal to ethnic or religious identity, and who usually controls a definable territory where he has a near monopoly on the use of force. A warlord, as opposed to a gang leader or petty crook, operates within a clear and defined political framework.

To bolster our state-building efforts in the future, we should instead look towards a British subaltern who in the early 20th century hastily scribbled some notes about the importance of warlords in the wastes of the Arabian Desert.

Lessons from Lawrence

Thomas Edward Lawrence, in the flower of his youth, was one of the most famous men in the world. The conqueror of Aqaba [town on the Gulf of Aqaba in what is now Jordan] at 29 and Damascus [capital of Syria] at thirty, he was a major leader of the wildly romantic and improbably successful Arab Revolt of Emir Feisal—a warlord—against his Turkish overlords during World War I. There is no doubting Lawrence's military achievement. During the Great War, 50,000 Turks were pinned down east of the Jordan by an Arab force of around 3,000 irregulars operating under his immediate direction. A further 150,000 Turks were spread over the rest of the region in a vain effort to crush the Arab Revolt, so little more than 50,000 were left to meet the assault by Sir Edmund Allenby—the senior British officer in theater and Lawrence's commanding general. The British historian and a friend of Lawrence's, Basil Liddell-Hart, noted that while it was unlikely that the Arab forces alone could have overcome the Turks without British assistance, it was equally true that Allenby could not have defeated the Turks without the Arabs and Lawrence.

Lawrence's approach was based on a few simple principles, encapsulated in an August 1917 memo he wrote for British

An Uncultured Military

The US has the wrong sort of military to engage the enemies it currently confronts, for it has the wrong sort of population whence to recruit soldiers. A hundred years ago just 3,000 British officers controlled the whole of the Indian subcontinent, but most of them commanded local troops in their own language. US Special Forces, as I observed in reviewing Robert Kaplan's book *Imperial Grunts* (*Do you call that an empire?* October 4, 2005), display nonpareil technical skill and valor in the field, but unlike the officer corps of the Indian Army, did not cut their teeth on Greek and Latin at school. . . .

The Israeli army can relegate skilled Arabic translators among its reservists to routine guard duty because Arabic is compulsory for Israeli secondary-school students. Americans lack the cultural depth to manage the welter of ethnicities and sects of the Middle East.

Sprangler, "How I Learned to Stop Worrying and Love Chaos,"
Asia Times *online, March 14, 2006. www.atimes.com.*

officers serving with Feisal's legions, and in a September 1920 article he wrote anonymously for the British journal *Round Table*. What Lawrence advocated in these primary sources represents a dramatic break not only with state-building as it was then practiced, but also as it continues to be implemented today.

Local elites, Lawrence held, must be stakeholders in any successful state-building process. At root, almost all state-building problems are political and not military in nature; with political legitimacy, military problems can be solved. To work against the grain of local history is to fail. It is critical to accurately assess the unit of politics in a developing state—and in the case of the Arab Revolt, it was the tribe, and hence tribal leaders, or warlords.

Working Within Ethnic Norms

To Lawrence, the seminal operational fact in dealing with the Arab Revolt was that the framework was tribal. By working within Bedouin cultural norms, rather than imposing Western institutions, the Arabs accepted the legitimacy of British objectives. As he wrote in his 1917 memo, "Wave a Sharif [local warlord] in front of you like a banner, and hide your own mind and person." Lawrence understood that the sharif, not he, had local legitimacy. The common British custom was to issue orders to the Arabs only through their chiefs, and only when agreed upon. Lawrence did not take this approach out of some romantic belief in the unspoiled ways of the Arabs. Rather, he saw it as the only practical way to achieve results. Lawrence worked with local culture, history, political practice, sociology, ethnology, economic statutes and psychology to get the job done.

Early on, Lawrence realized that in Emir Feisal he had happened upon the ideal warlord of the Arab Revolt. As son of the sharif of Mecca [holiest site in Islam, now in Saudi Arabia], Feisal was imbued with religious and political legitimacy. He led in the name of his father, who as keeper of the Holy Places had an unrivalled political position in the Hejaz (western Saudi Arabia). Lawrence worked within the tribal structure and collaborated with warlords, an approach he employed later on his way to Damascus, when he successfully constructed another alliance of Syrian tribes, including the Howeitat, Beni Sakhr, Sherrat, Rualla and Serahin.

The contrast with modern Western efforts at state-building could hardly be greater. Too often, modern-day Wilsonians assume that because a nation-state exists on paper, they can dispense with the need to forge alliances and compacts among sectarian, tribal, ethnic and religious factions and simply deal with "Iraqis" or "Somalis" or "Afghans"—disregarding or ignoring the traditional sub-national centers of authority in favor of anointing "modern" leaders. . . .

Enlightened Warlordism

More than any other country, Afghanistan has been shaped by warlordism—and has paid a steep price for it. In the past quarter-century, this battlefield of empires was shattered by two decades of conflict, first against the Soviet Union and its proxies, and then after 1989 as the victorious warlords jockeyed to fill the power gap. Far from an anomaly, those episodes were the newest chapter in Afghanistan's longer history of fratricidal warfare and hopeless governance, which some commentators attribute to the country's complex DNA. ([Author and leading expert on Afghanistan] Barnett Rubin even speaks of an environment of "competitive state-building.") Save for a few distinct attempts at national edification (such as under the rule of Amir Abd al-Rahman's from 1880 to 1901, or under the Taliban), legitimacy in Afghanistan has remained with the warlords and their sponsors. From the mid-17th century to today, outside powers—Persia, Russia, Britain, and finally the Soviet Union and the United States—have at one point or another leveraged Afghanistan's sectarian and ethnic fabric for their own benefits.

The talent of the Bush Administration was not to face the reality of Afghanistan's warlordism or merely manage it—they had no choice—but to embrace it, to use it fully and shrewdly as a powerful instrument for nation-building. "Afghanistan" would have to be cobbled together with the same tools the Carolingians [dynasty of French rulers] and General [Giuseppe] Garibaldi [Italian military officer whose battles led to a unified Italy] had used with France and Italy: guns, bribes, patience . . . and a little prayer. U.S. policy benefited to some degree from Washington's benign neglect of Afghanistan. U.S. officials working there were forced into pragmatism due to the lack of resources and attention. Washington's distaste for warlords was much more evident and consequential in Iraq, due to America's more singular and detrimental focus there.

At the time Kabul was turned over to a U.S.-led coalition in late 2001, the Taliban [fundamentalist Islamists who ruled Afghanistan from 1996 to 2001] regime gave way to a mosaic of around two-dozen major ethnic and tribal warlords. The United Islamic Front for the Salvation of Afghanistan, as the Northern Alliance was officially known, was a coalition of ethnic warlords, the most important of whom were Abdul Rashid Dostum, an Uzbek, and Mohamed Daoud Fahim, the successor to Ahmed Shah Masoud, and Ustad Mohamed Atta, both Tadjiks. This group also included several smaller Hazara (Shi'a) [Muslim religious and political group] factions. In the east and southeast, around two-dozen Pashtun [ethnic groups in the border region between Afghanistan and Pakistan] warlords were competing—often violently—to fill the power vacuum left by the Taliban. (The CIA's own warlords in the region were busier fighting each other than chasing Osama bin Laden in Tora Bora [white mountain region of western Afghanistan] in late 2001.) The south and west were under the firm control, respectively, of Gul Agha Sherza (a supporter of the late king, Zahir Shah), and Herat's [city in western Afghanistan] Iran-backed strongman Ismail Khan.

U.S. to Warlords: Evolve or Die

By demonstrating to the warlords its extraordinary might and firepower during the course of Operation Enduring Freedom, the United States simply imposed itself as Afghanistan's most powerful and most ruthless warlord and designated Hamid Karzai, no matter what his official title was in international circles, as its representative. While having lived in exile for some of the twenty years before the U.S. intervention in Afghanistan, Karzai—as a prominent member of the powerful Pashtun Popalzay clan—had remained a fairly powerful player in Afghanistan's Pashtun community. He had been a very efficient fund-raiser in Afghanistan and Pakistan during the anti-Soviet jihad [holy war] in the 1980s and had even played a very important role in the initial creation of the Taliban in the early 1990s. In many ways, Karzai was the anti-Chalabi [Ahmed Chalabi, leader of the exiled Iraqi National Congress, formed in 1992 to overthrow Saddam Hussein].

Meanwhile, by opening the December 2001 Bonn Conference [Bonn, Germany meeting among influential Afghans, the UN and United States to reproduce Afghanistan as a nation after the U.S. 2001 invasion] to the warlords and their sponsors (including Iran), the United States government laid the foundation of a broad-based strategy involving a simple but existential bargain with the warlords: Evolve or die. Operate through a reasonably democratic political process and contribute to the edification of a united, stable Afghanistan and you will survive—albeit as a lesser entity. Or wait for the B-52s.

With a few minor exceptions, Afghanistan's powerful factions matched America's pragmatism and agreed to support Hamid Karzai—a Pashtun—and his Afghan Interim Authority.

Beginning in 2002 they were tacitly allowed to consolidate and even increase their private armies, their regional power base and, most important, their own sources of revenue (opium or customs). Against the tacit promise to turn this power into democratic legitimacy and loyalty to the central government, they were even allowed to "cash in" their authority in the new Afghanistan by taking active responsibility in Karzai's administration. Regardless of their democratic credentials or human rights record, many Afghan warlords were elevated to positions of authority at the national and local levels.

This was by no means a smooth process. Regional warlords displeased with new hierarchies have clashed over authority and territory. At the same time, some non-Pashtun officials in the new administration became mistrustful of Karzai's philosophy of ethnic equality, especially in regards to building the Afghan National Army. Others, such as Ismail Khan, re-sisted accepting a diminished role and were reluctant to share real power with the central government. So while there have been some important positive developments for Karzai's ad-ministration, this issue of regional control—especially with re-gard to fiscal and military matters—remains very much on top of the agenda for successfully moving Afghanistan through the next phases of its nation-building.

While the warlords have been bribed and coerced into not hijacking the future of Afghanistan, they have yet to fully rec-oncile their authority with a commitment to peace and stabil-ity. But the warlords have made a crucial first step toward channeling their identity, authority and regional conflicts of interest through a non-violent, national and democratic pro-cess. They have been allowed to think that their legitimacy could safely be transferred from the barrels of their guns to the support of their constituents, especially in the areas and communities fearing the domination of Afghanistan by Pash-tuns.

The result is a country with a fragile democratic consensus and a largely uncertain future, but one with a genuine chance for stability that the Bush Administration cannot even afford to dream about in Iraq.

Working with Warlords

Given the continued relevance of the oft-maligned warlord, how should the United States work with them while engaging in state-building? Here what ought to have been done in Iraq illustrates Lawrence's alternative model of working with local elites, democratically elected or not. Instead of fretting about interim constitutions, permanent constitutions and finding the George Washington of Iraq, a better approach would have involved establishing a loose confederation—where all the ma-jor units of political expression (Kurds [natives of northern Iraq], Sunni [minority Islamic political group in Iraq] and

Shi'a) and their warlords were represented in the central government and given broad local autonomy.

In Iraq and other countries, communicating the language of common U.S. and warlord interests would be best. The administration should have assured the leaders of the three communities that a federal political system is the best means of ensuring local autonomy, protecting against the return of a tyrannical central government, and equitably disbursing Iraq's oil and tax revenues. A decentralized system, given the organic nature of Iraq's indigenous politics, always was most likely to fit political realities on the ground, suit the warlords and meet the needs of Iraq's people.

Instead of mindlessly droning on about democracy, a more genuinely moral rule should always guide American efforts at state-building: The United States should leave developing countries better off than they found them. After all, stability is central to long-term political success. In order to do so, it is imperative to work with local elites—and this includes the warlords—to ensure the stability that is so vital to any state-building enterprise. The warlord of Indiana Jones's day may be a laughable and slightly repulsive creature. In the real world, he is the key to moving toward a model for statecraft that stands a chance of success. American efforts at state-building, and the War on Terror itself, begin and end in Washington. It is there that significant changes in thinking must be made.

| "Most people in Afghanistan live under the effective rule of warlords whose only merit may be that they are opponents of the Taleban. In every other respect, they are indistinguishable from the Taleban."

Nation-Building with Warlords Is Not Justified

John Chuckman

John Chuckman argues that much of Afghanistan lives as if it were rooted in the 14th century, controlled by regional warlords who are the de facto leaders of the country, no matter what democratic principles nation-builders try to convey through the government in Kabul, the country's capital. The author believes the warlords have corrupted the American democratic mission in Afghanistan. John Chuckman writes for the Politics Canada *Web site.*

As you read, consider the following questions:

    1. The author believes the term "nation-building" is absurd. What does he give as reasons for this belief?

John Chuckman, "The Parable of the Hatchet or the Nonsense of Nation-Building in Afghanistan," *Politics Canada*, November 3, 2006. Reproduced by permission of the author.

2. How much influence does the president of Afghanistan Hamad Karzai have outside the capital city, Kabul, according to Chuckman?

3. Who did a better job promoting modern changes in Afghanistan, especially for women, than the United States and its warlord allies, according to the viewpoint author?

Nation-building is a term created by people living off Pentagon contracts. It is one of those queasy political expressions with no hard meaning yet its use raises few eyebrows.

The term sounds as though it means something, and it is treated as though it were something you might study. At least this is true in the United States where people are hypnotized by hype and substance-lacking words, where inflating nothing into something is an everyday art.

The Absurdity of Nation-Building

To understand what absurdity the term disguises, conduct a brief thought-experiment and think about just one aspect of social behavior in North America and about how long it takes to change. Cigarette smoking was very stylish fifty years ago, and it has taken all those fifty years, despite scientific information providing many warnings, to change public acceptance of smoking.

In 19th century America, chewing tobacco and spitting were obsessions, observed and recorded by many disturbed European visitors. Spittoons graced the halls and lobbies of every public building, standing in ripples of warm brown carpet stains where the efforts of the less skilled were recorded. Eventually, this hideous practice ended, but it took a very long time.

So how much greater would be the task of altering the most fundamental attitudes and practices in a society? Could even ten years of costly effort by thousands hope to make even a small dent in the practices of an ancient society of twenty million people?

Stuck in the 14th Century

Much of Afghanistan lives as though it were still the 14th century, and this is the case any place where there has been little economic growth for centuries, where people grow up doing pretty much exactly what their parents do.

In Western society of the 14th century, it was perfectly acceptable for men to go off to war, leaving their mates locked in rude iron "chastity belts" with padlocks for years at a time. In Western society of the 14th century, it was common practice among powerful families to contract a 12-year old girl to marriage. Is the practice of women wearing the bourka [traditional fundamentalist Muslim clothing covering the entire body] in Afghanistan somehow more primitive than the past customs of Europe?

I take the bourka as an example only because a great many words were spent both before and after the invasion about the status of women in Iraq. Most of this was sheer hypocrisy, propaganda aimed at influencing the attitudes of America's middle class in favor of war. As I've written many times, truth makes the best propaganda—it's all a matter of twisting emphasis and context. Today, outside the city of Kabul, almost all women still wear the bourka, and it has nothing to do with threats from the Taleban. Even in Kabul half the women wear it.

Warlords Are Here to Stay

The distinction between Kabul and the rest of Afghanistan is important, because the effective reach of Afghanistan's president [Hamid Karzai] has been compared to that of a Mayor of Kabul. Most people in Afghanistan live under the effective rule of warlords whose only merit may be that they are oppo-

Rehabilitating the Warlords

The Afghan civil war during the Taliban rule had another dimension: the warlords. The warlords humiliated, coerced and murdered tens of thousands of Afghans, and most of them had a narrow support base in their immediate ethnic or tribal communities. The United States, by co-opting them as allies against the Taliban, rehabilitated them, empowered them with money and weapons and gave them a dignified space in the new political structure.

Most of them have committed untellable atrocities against their political and ethnic rivals and could be put before an international criminal tribunal for their crimes against humanity. All of them have been spared for the "good" work they have done for the US and ISAF forces. If the resolution of the lower house of the Afghan parliament is passed by the upper house, all of them will be granted amnesty. This may set a bad example and encourage the same lot and others to raise militias and acquire enough power to bargain for influence and recognition.

Rasul Bakhsh Rais, "Afghanistan's Falling War," Daily Times, February 6, 2007. www.dailytimes.com.

nents of the Taleban. In every other respect, they are indistinguishable from the Taleban. They hate seeing women without bourkas. They do not like girls going to public school. They do not believe in democracy—who did in Europe in the 14th century?—and they reject modern concepts of human rights.

The warlords, at least some of them, finance their satrapies with the proceeds of poppy crops, causing an explosion in the world's supply of high-grade heroin, the Taleban, for all their unpleasant qualities, having previously ended this trade. The warlords are torturers and murderers, and their militias are capable of almost any horror you can imagine, some having conducted mass rapes according to numerous witnesses.

Yet the warlords cannot be removed. They were an integral part of the American strategy for invading Afghanistan, and they remain pillars of the existing state. America's strategy consisted of bombing the Taleban and their supporters while warlord militias did most of the dirty work on the ground. America sent in thousands of special forces to search the mountains for Osama bin Laden and remnant Taleban bands, but for the most part they have been no more successful than the Russians were years ago. They have been successful in alienating and insulting many villagers with their tactics of bursting in with guns and grenades firing.

Apart from having killed thousands with bombs and mines, this is pretty much the sum total of America's achievement in Afghanistan. The Russians actually had done a better job of making secular changes, especially for women, but this was ignored in American propaganda to win support for the CIA's costly mujahideen [Muslim warrior]-proxy war, the war that gave us figures like Osama bin Laden and led to the eventual rule of the Taleban.

The 14th Century Meets the 21st

A Canadian officer in Afghanistan recently was gravely injured when a young man attacked him with a home-made ax. The officer had removed his helmet out of respect towards the village elders to whom he was talking. The young Afghan man was immediately killed by other Canadian soldiers. Newspapers typically reported his age as maybe 20. In fact, it turns out he was only 16. A brief exchange of gun fire with some others who produced weapons then occurred.

The incident provides something of a parable for the entire misadventure in Afghanistan. First, the soldier was right to remove his helmet. You can't get far in a society like Afghanistan without showing respect.

Second, a young man of just 16 was determined to take the life of a foreigner despite his lack of a suitable weapon and despite the likelihood of his sacrificing his life.

Third, because it was a small village, there is no possibility that the elders who were gathered were not aware of the impending assault. They kept silent and allowed it to happen.

Fourth, one of the reactions to the assault has been for Canadian officials to re-examine their practices, things like a soldier removing his helmet. Yet how can they hope to be sympathetically listened to otherwise? The alternative is to follow America's apish tactics, creating even more bitter enemies. It is an unavoidable vicious circle.

Undistinguished Nation-Building

Canadians and others find themselves in Afghanistan because a brutal American administration, in the wake of 9/11 [the September 11, 2001 terrorist attacks on the United States], instead of using diplomatic and legal powers to capture Osama and the boys, pressured everyone to support an invasion. Canada was later able to resist pressure for the even more pointless and destructive invasion of Iraq. Canadians today are asking what is the purpose of the mission in Afghanistan. The answers offered include that empty term, nation-building.

> *"The Bush administration seems to think that it has learned the lessons of Somalia by not messing with the warlords and by leaving the nation-building to others. This is simply wrong."*

Nation-Building Must Confront Warlords to Be Justified

Sarah Sewall

Sarah Sewall was deputy assistant secretary of defense for peacekeeping in the Clinton administration, and is program director at the Carr Center for Human Rights Policy at Harvard University. In this viewpoint, she argues that America has failed to confront regional warlords during nation-building ever since the failed U.N.–U.S. operation in Somalia. Sewall declares that nations such as Afghanistan cannot be effectively rebuilt with warlords creating chaos and securing their own interests to the detriment of their nation.

As you read, consider the following questions:

1. Why was accommodating the Somalia warlords such a drastic mistake, according to Sewall?

2. To face up to Afghanistan's security requirements, what action does Sewall recommend with regards to warlords?

3. It is time for America to stop using the U.N. for what, according to the viewpoint author?

By insisting that the United Nations do the "dirty work" of nation-building without ensuring a secure foundation upon which to build, President George W. Bush is effectively setting up the UN to fail in Afghanistan, much as his father's [President George H.W. Bush] policies sowed the seeds for failure in Somalia. The US refusal to support disarming and defusing the warlord culture renders even the most effective nation-building efforts a Band-Aid at best.

Accommodating warlords was the linchpin of the initial US intervention strategy in Somalia. This pragmatic approach acknowledged the reality of factionalism in that lawless country. There was only one problem. It failed to weaken the fiefdoms that had torn the country apart. No matter, as long as the United States wanted to drop off food and get out. But it mattered enormously when the UN was asked to help create a functioning state.

Failure to Secure the Warlord

The UN mission was placed at risk by a Somali warlord [Mohamed Farrah Aidid] who decided that the foreign peacekeepers had become a liability. The UN lacked the requisite capabilities to confront him. A US operation went bad, Americans died, and the entire UN effort unraveled. Somalia largely reverted to its pre-intervention lawlessness. US officials now speak of terrorist cells and other threats gestating in the chaos that is Somalia today [as of this writing].

At the time, critics saw the UN peacekeeping effort in Somalia as proof that nation-building was a mistake. However, the real failure in Somalia was not nation-building per se, but the failure to first create a secure foundation on which other efforts would depend.

Warlord Nation

Experts call Somalia a failed state. This is a sophism. Somalia was a failed state in 1990 under the last central government of the mildly insane Mohamed Siad Barre. Nowadays, one could call Somalia a space between countries. Or simply a feral nation. This is the place that perfected the practice of extorting cash from international aid organizations in return for allowing the aid groups the privilege of feeding other starving Somalis. (Gangsters R Us, with Third World panache.) When the United Nations tried to intervene and establish a central government in 1993 (an admittedly naive effort), the Somalis united just long enough to drive off the foreigners and resume their embrace of warlords and clans.

Garrett Jones, "The Next Horror in Somalia,"
Los Angeles Times, *December 10, 2006. www.latimes.com.*

The United States Can't Outsource Security

Security is a precondition for political reform, economic development, and other aspects of what is pejoratively termed "nation-building." (It was called "postwar reconstruction" when we did it for Europe, where it was considered both self-serving and heroic.) Even the most energetic and well-resourced efforts cannot construct a nation amid the shifting sands of unaccountable, well-armed mini despots.

In Afghanistan [in 2002], [former] Deputy Defense Secretary Paul D. Wolfowitz calls regional powers with a great deal of autonomy a matter of Afghan culture. He warns against intervening too actively on behalf of the central government for fear that people may become too reliant upon that intervention.

This classic conservative suspicion about government, which lies at the heart of objections to nation-building, seems curiously misapplied to nations long suffering from the absence of government. How can Afghanistan hope for a different future if nation-building simply augments power structures of the past? The Bush administration seems to think that it has learned the lessons of Somalia by not messing with the warlords and by leaving the nation-building to others. This is simply wrong.

Stabilizing a Warlord Culture

Confronting the warlords is neither easy nor the best use of American troops at this moment [in 2002]. Our most pressing security concerns lie elsewhere. But the peace in Afghanistan is fragile at best. It can be undone by the concerted efforts of one nasty regional leader. And its undoing will have significant costs.

For reconstruction to proceed, for any hope of future stability, there must be a modicum of security beyond Kabul. If the Afghan central government cannot do this (which is doubtful in the near term), a capable, neutral force that can disarm and dissuade the warlords is vital. No one wants to contemplate the numbers, the capabilities, the costs required. But it is unrealistic to expect sustainable progress without facing up to the country's security requirements.

Ensure the Possibility for Success

It is time for the United States to stop using the UN simply to provide our forces with an exit strategy and to keep American hands unsullied by nation-building. The US government should either create the possibilities for peace before asking others to maintain it, or the administration should support follow-on forces that are up to the challenge they will face.

We need to learn the right lessons from past failures. Before handing off our responsibilities, we should ensure some possibility of success for those who would help clean up the mess.

Periodical Bibliography

The following articles have been selected to supplement the diverse views presented in this chapter.

Michael Barone   "The Pentagon's New Map," *US News & World Report*, May 20, 2004, www.usnews.com.

Alejandro Benana   "From Peace-Building to State-Building: One Step Forward and Two Backwards?" *Centro de Estudios Internacionales*, October 15, 2004, www.ceinicaragua.org.

Christian Bundegaard   "The Battalion State: Securitization and Nation-Building in Eritrea," *Programme for Strategic and International Security Studies* (PSIS), 2004, www.psis.org.

Noam Chomsky   "US–Haiti," *Znet*, March 2004, www.zmag.org.

Mark Jason Gilbert   "Fatal Amnesia: American Nation-Building in Vietnam, Afghanistan, and Iraq," *Journal of Third World Studies*, Fall 2004.

Ameen Izzadeen   "In Nepal, Democracy á la Shangri-la," *The Sunday Times Online*, January 21, 2007, http://sundaytimes.lk.

Salma Malik and   "Small Arms and the Security Debate in South
Mallika Joseph   Asia," *Institute of Peace and Conflict Studies*, 2004, www.ipcs.org.

Rajan Menon   "Afghanistan's Minor Miracle," *Los Angeles Times*, December 14, 2004, www.latimes.com.

Bruce Patterson   "Disappeared," *Anderson Valley Advertiser*, June 21, 2006, www.theava.com.

Roy Ratnarel   "MAD," *Sangam.org*, Association of Tamils of Sri Lanka in the USA, July 4, 2006, www.sangam.org.

Anne-Marie Slaughter   "Democrat Foreign Policy Take 2: Neo-Colonialists Versus Sensible Realists?" *America Abroad: Notes on Foreign Affairs, TPM Café*, January 16, 2006, www.tpmcafe.com.

CHAPTER 2

Can Nation-Building Combat Terrorism?

Chapter Preface

President George W. Bush announced in 2007 that he was reading Alistair Horne's book *A Savage War of Peace*, which is about the French war in the North African country of Algeria from 1954 to 1962. Observers noted that the story posed eerie similarities to the U.S. predicament in Iraq in 2007.

On November 1, 1954, the National Liberation Front for Algeria (FLN—Front de Libération Nationale) launched dawn raids on colonial French military posts and infrastructure throughout Algeria. France had run Algeria as its colony since 1830. The FLN demanded, via a radio message broadcast from Cairo, Egypt, the "restoration of the Algerian state, sovereign, democratic, and social, within the framework of the principles of Islam." France's minister of the interior, socialist Francois Mitterand, answered the FLN by saying, "the only possible negotiation is war."

Algerian nationalists formed an insurgency that attacked, using terror and guerrilla methods, French and Algerian administrators, military, police, and worse—in the eyes of the world—innocent civilians. French farmers and landowners in Algeria fled from the country's interior to the capital city of Algiers. They pressured the French government to halt the revolt. The French responded by detaining suspected insurgents in mass sweeps, which the French knew would include innocents. The Algerian suspects were jailed without a court hearing and interrogations included physical and mental torture.

The French media published numerous articles on the Algerian tortures. Although the French people had initially supported the war, the media reports, coupled with mounting French and civilian casualties, and a growing revulsion toward colonialism, helped induce a climate of outrage and a groundswell of public opposition to the war. France eventually negotiated a treaty with Algeria. French elections in June 1962 approved Algerian independence by a 91 percent mandate. Historians and participants calculate the war's death toll between 300,000 to one million people.

France's Algerian war and America's occupation of Iraq obviously bear some similarities. Insurgents in both wars were, and are, fundamentally Muslim and believed Islam should be the foundation of their societies. France became mediator and combatant in what, many historians concluded, was simultaneously a civil war and an anticolonial, terrorist insurgency. America appears to be facing the same situation in Iraq. Algerian and Iraqi Muslims fought on both sides in their respective conflicts. Both occupiers, France and the United States, had and have difficulty identifying and separating terrorists from ordinary citizens. Reconstruction contractors in Iraq cite security as the number one problem in rebuilding the country.

The French and United States both detained and tortured prisoners to gain intelligence—the United States, most notably, at the Iraq prison Abu Ghraib and, some would say, at Guantánamo Bay, Cuba, where alleged terrorist combatants were being held indefinitely by the United States. Media revelations of torture caused growing public discontent toward both missions. Both countries had large in-country military complexes, assisted by large foreign affairs and diplomatic detachments. The borders of Algeria and Iraq are equally porous, allowing importing and exporting of reconstruction aid and indigenously produced products, as well as weapons and the movement of insurgents across the border.

Though Algeria is not Iraq, the similarities are sufficiently close that President George W. Bush would want to read about the Algerian crisis and how it might apply to America's attempts at nation-building in Iraq while fighting terrorist insurgents. In the chapter that follows, the authors argue, in opposing viewpoints, whether nation-building can combat terrorism.

> "The new GWOT [Global War on Ter-
> ror] era demands leaders who can fight
> as well as their Cold War predecessors
> could but who can also transition
> quickly and effectively to stability op-
> erations and nationbuilding to defeat
> radical Islam and its proselytizing ter-
> rorists."

Nation-Building Can Combat Terrorism

Patrick J. Donahoe

*Lieutenant Colonel Patrick J. Donahoe is professor of Security,
Strategy, and Force Planning at the U.S. Naval War College. In
this viewpoint, Donahoe argues that nation-building can combat
the global war on terror if U.S. Army officers are properly trained
in the dual functions of soldier and state-builder. The new army,
he argues, must be trained in high-intensity combat operations
and the ability to quickly transition to nation-building capabilities, utilizing a skill set that includes knowledge of the culture in
which U.S. forces are embedded.*

Patrick J. Donahoe, "Preparing Leaders for Nationbuilding," *The U.S. Army Professional Writing Collection*, June 2004. www.army.mil. Reproduced by permission.

As you read, consider the following questions:

1. The U.S. Army trains its force in combat operations while neglecting training in other areas, according to the author. What are those areas?

2. According to General Anthony Zinni, what responsibilities did U.S. Army leaders have to juggle in Iraq and Afghanistan, according to the viewpoint?

3. Why is it crucial to U.S. Army success to understand civics as part of nation-building, according to Donahoe?

In a [2003] article, author Robert Kaplan set forth 10 rules for "Managing the World." The first rule is "Produce More Joppolos," referring to Major Victor Joppolo, the protagonist of John Hersey's 1945 Pulitzer Prize–winning novel, *A Bell for Adano*. In Kaplan's view, the fictional Major Joppolo can serve as the model for soldiers during military occupations and peacemaking operations. We clearly need more Joppolos, he says and asks, where are they?

The United States has been waging the Global War on Terrorism (GWOT) since shortly after 11 September 2001 and, arguably, has been unofficially at war with terrorists since the end of Operation Desert Storm [in 1991]. U.S. involvements in international conflicts in the past decade demonstrate that the U.S. Army needs leaders who can shift quickly from combat to stability operations and back again with an eye on winning both war and peace in the Islamic Middle East battlespace. The Army trains the force across the spectrum of conflict but focuses most of its training efforts on high-intensity combat operations while ignoring training on cultural, civic, ethical, and city planning duties that soldiers must perform in Iraq and elsewhere.

The Army must train its leaders to adapt to a fundamentally changed security environment. While the Cold War demanded Army leaders who could lead formations into battle, the new GWOT era demands leaders who can fight as well as their Cold War predecessors could but who can also transition quickly and effectively to stability operations and nationbuilding to defeat radical Islam and its proselytizing terrorists.

Winning Hearts and Minds

In Iraq and elsewhere, the Army asks battalion and company combat commanders to conduct nationbuilding and act as civil affairs officers. Soldiers must master warfighting skills to seize and secure terrain and towns while working peacefully with the local populace and, hopefully, persuading them that nonviolence is the best path to stability. Failing to win the hearts and minds of local people might not sound a mission's death knell, but it makes success in suppressing insurgencies and terrorism more difficult. What is the Army doing to prepare leaders for these undertakings?

In Hersey's story, Joppolo is the archetype for the U.S. military officer or senior noncommissioned officer (NCO) who finds himself working with the "natives" after a successful military campaign. The Army transformed Joppolo, an Italian-American clerk from the Bronx, into a civil affairs officer and assigned him to follow combat troops into Italy during World War II. Eventually he became the military mayor of an Italian town.

After the invasion and liberation of Italy, Joppolo became the face of the American Military Government of Occupied Territories to the people of Adano, Sicily, a small seaside fishing village. A fair-minded man intent on being a just and well-liked city administrator, Joppolo worked diligently at settling Adano's internal disputes, including punishing the village's former mayor, a fascist. Joppolo received permission from the U.S. Navy for local fishermen to return to sea to earn their livelihood. Joppolo's final task was to find a replacement for Adano's bell, which Italian Fascist [and Italy's leader during WWII] Benito Mussolini's soldiers had melted down for armaments.

Building Army Jugglers

Joppolo had certain advantages that today's Army peacemakers in Iraq do not have. As an Italian-American, he was fluent in Italian, understood Italian culture, and had a personal connection to Italy. Today's Joppolo is an infantryman or tanker who does not have Joppolo's training and skills and faces an incredibly steep learning curve to successfully execute his mission. Still, Army commanders in the field in Iraq expect to be as successful as Joppolo was, even though they do not speak the language, have little understanding of the culture in which they are immersed, and have no personal connection to the country. Also, the Army expects combat arms officers and NCOs to accomplish the tasks that Joppolo as a trained civil affairs specialist performed. The Army has been unsuccessful in recruiting adequate numbers of Afghani- or Iraqi-Americans to fill its ranks of civil affairs officers and cannot conscript them to do so.

Retired U.S. Central Command Commander General Anthony Zinni described the challenges facing the Army's new Joppolos in a recent speech: "On one hand, you have to shoot and kill somebody; on the other hand, you have to feed somebody. On the other hand, you have to build an economy, restructure the infrastructure, and build the political system. And there's some poor lieutenant colonel, colonel, brigadier general down there, stuck in some province with all that saddled onto him, with NGOs [nongovernmental organizations] and political wannabes running around, with factions and a culture he doesn't understand." Such conflicts are occurring today, and these responsibilities are being juggled right now in Iraq and Afghanistan.

Today, artillery battery commanders and cavalry troop commanders are interacting with local politicians and religious leaders, and many of them are doing rather well. The Army needs to equip them with better skills to make them more effective, however. The Army cannot draft men like Vic-

Wave and Smile

One of the most important ways in which the New Zealand team implemented its mission was to build convivial and constructive relationships with the local Afghan communities. It was emphasised to teams to always wave and smile wherever they went and this soon resulted in communities similarly waving and smiling back. Simple things like removing reflective sunglasses when talking to people made the teams appear more accessible and less aloof or arrogant. Teams stopped and spoke with community elders, and while team leaders explained why they were there, what they were doing and ascertained community security issues, soldiers would be playing with a frizbee, a ball or even simple 'Simon says' with the children outside. It was most reassuring to hear peels of laughter from the children outside when the soldiers did something funny to entertain the children. This is where the real hearts and minds were won. Although simple, indeed some might say trite, it is an essential component of gaining trust, respect, co-operation and support. Afghans are extremely hospitable and would always invite teams in for tea and invite them to stay for lunch or dinner or even the night.

Peter Nichols, "Fighting Terrorism in Afghanistan,"
New Zealand International Review, *March 1, 2006.*

tor Joppolo, so it must build them. The Army must also educate officers and senior NCOs about the culture, language, history, and geography of the civilizations in which they will operate. The [Army] III Corps embarked on such training before deploying to Iraq in 2003. The Army needs to include training in Middle East culture; basic law and civics; city planning and public administration; economics; and ethics in officer basic and career courses, advanced NCO courses, and at the U.S.

Army Sergeants Major Academy to prepare leaders for the challenges they will face in Iraq and Afghanistan.

Cultural Immersion

If modern-day Joppolos are to relate successfully to Iraqis or Afghanis, they must have a basic understanding of the country's history, language, and culture. As the U.S. Marine Corps (USMC) *Small Wars Manual* says, "Knowledge of the character of the people and a command of their language are great assets." Ironically, the Army did this throughout the Cold War in Germany. Many soldiers received a 2-week immersion in the culture of Germany through the Head Start program where they learned about the German language and culture when they arrived in Europe.

The Middle East—the Tigris and Euphrates River valleys in particular—is said to be the cradle of civilization, and the Iraqis, Kuwaitis, and Iranians who live there are proud and distinct peoples. If American soldiers do not respect Arab, Persian, and Afghan social customs, they could create an atmosphere of antagonism. Soldiers must understand and have a civilized respect for Islamic traditions and religious beliefs, including the differing beliefs of Sunni, Shiite, and other sects.

Army leaders should be familiar with the languages spoken in their probable areas of operations. The advanced NCO courses, the basic and career officer courses, and the staff and war colleges should provide language training. Officers and NCOs should be able to choose early in their careers to focus on languages that are of greatest use to the Army. At a minimum, the Army should provide Berlitz-type language tapes to its leaders now rather than waiting until they deploy. The USMC understood this in the 1930s and put it in their Small Wars Manual: "If not already familiar with the language, all officers upon assignment to expeditionary duty should study and acquire a working knowledge of it." As Chief of Staff of the Army General Peter J. Schoomaker has said, the Army needs an expeditionary mindset. Language training should be a part of it.

Victorian England had men who understood the ancient cultures of the Middle East. Among these men were T.E. Lawrence, who gained fame as Lawrence of Arabia, and Colonel Orde Wingate, who spent most of his adult life living in Egypt. The modern U.S. Army has few combat arms officers who have lived and worked among the Arabs for years. A cadre of foreign area officers with career field designation exists, but it is composed of people who never returned to combat units after they attained the rank of captain. Combat arms officers, if they have experience with Arabs at all, gained it during 1-year postings to Saudi Arabia or Kuwait.

One personnel management policy that could give combat arms officers more exposure to the Middle East would be an enhanced exchange program requiring officers to serve 6-month or 1-year tours with foreign armies around the world. The Army will probably be rotating forces into and out of the Muslim world for at least another decade. Even if not, it is prudent to prepare for the eventuality.

Knowing How to Run a City

Army officers should understand the legal structures they might have to resurrect, revitalize, or reinstall in foreign countries. Many battalion-level commanders and some company-level commanders will be intimately involved in setting up or supervising legal systems and activities in Iraq and Afghanistan. Law and civics classes are essential to preparing leaders for this duty. Legal training is imperative. Army leaders must understand their legal obligations and the judicial systems that America wants to see emerge. Understanding civics is critical to the success of these operations. Promoting democracy in the Middle East and Afghanistan will be quite difficult if Army leaders do not have a working knowledge of a democratic government's organizations and functions. When the Army directs its soldiers to play Joppolo and govern towns and cities in an occupied territory, soldiers must know how a free, democratic government is supposed to work.

Knowing how to run a city is essential to establishing safety and stability in an urban environment. The most pressing problems Army troops initially faced in Iraq were the reestablishment of electric power, and providing clean water and health care services. Soldiers must understand the basic functions of city administration and how to organize public works departments to maintain, fix, and if necessary, establish basic city services. The vitality of the local economy and the ability of citizens to buy, sell, and transport goods are essential for a return to normalcy. Freely exchanging goods and services and distributing food (outside of emergency governmental aid) are critical to security.

From Combat to Ethics

The American people, the international community, and the laws of land warfare demand that U.S. forces treat prisoners humanely. Many senior officers comment on the problems inherent in complying with the Geneva Conventions and the Law of Armed Conflict, but soldiers must understand the power of these laws to help the Nation prevail against guerrillas and insurgents. Leaders must understand the adverse effects that violations of these rules have on the soldiers under their command and on the enemy. In 2003, Lieutenant Colonel Allen B. West, an artillery battalion commander, was relieved of command for discharging his weapon near an Iraqi prisoner of war in order to elicit information from him. West's actions demonstrate that tactical leaders do not always clearly understand what is ethical behavior and what is not.

Because U.S. troops will continue to deploy to foreign lands and involvement in the Middle East might continue for some time, the Army needs leaders who can shift quickly from combat to stability operations. The Army must ensure that its leaders have the intellectual and physical tools to succeed as de facto civil affairs officers. The Army needs more leaders like Major Victor Joppolo.

> *"A realist approach to combating terror-
> ism . . . does not hinge on nation build-
> ing or making the world safe for de-
> mocracy."*

Nation-Building Cannot Combat Terrorism

Gary T. Dempsey

*Gary T. Dempsey is a foreign policy analyst at the Cato Institute
and editor of the book* Exiting the Balkan Thicket. *Dempsey argues in this viewpoint that nation-building actually detracts
from the problem of fighting terrorism. He analyzes factors that
nation-builders claim are the best reasons for such interventions,
and proposes that they are inherently bad reasons to intervene
and poorer choices for fighting the global war on terror.*

As you read, consider the following questions:

1. The author claims that as of 2002, there are 106 countries with oppressive or semi-oppressive governments.
   What percentage of the world's population, using this
   calculation, are potential targets for nation-building,
   according to Dempsey?

2. Many current notions of the root causes of terrorism are flawed, according to Dempsey. What are these false assumptions about the root causes of terrorism, according to the author?

3. Dempsey claims that Afghanistan was relatively stable from about 1930 to 1978. What led to the disruption of internal Afghan politics and the emergence of the fundamentalist Islamic Taliban government, according to the author?

Since September 11, 2001, there have been calls from various quarters to embrace nation building as a tool for combating terrorism. The logic behind the idea is that "good" states do not do "bad" things, so Washington should build more "good" states. That idea, however, relies on several dubious assumptions—for example, that embarking on multiple nation-building missions will reduce the potential for anti-American terrorism. If anything, nation building is likely to create more incentives, targets, and opportunities for terrorism, not fewer. The nation-building idea also draws on false analogies with the past. For example, some people assert that Europe's experience under the Marshall Plan [U.S. plan to rebuild Europe post-WWII] can be readily duplicated in a whole host of countries and that, with enough economic aid, trained bureaucrats, and military force of arms, "bad" states anywhere can be transformed into open, serf-sustaining, peaceful states.

In reality, combating terrorism is tied to the realist perspective, which says that it increasingly makes sense for states to use or condone violence, including terrorism when they fall prey to the idea that violence will succeed. A realist approach to combating terrorism, therefore, does not hinge on nation building or making the world safe for democracy. It hinges on a policy of victory and credible deterrence. And if there is no competent government for the United States to deter? U.S.

policymakers should understand that that is precisely where the terrorists are at their most vulnerable, because there is no power to protect them. . . .

Calculating Reality

Osama bin Laden's al-Qaeda organization, which was responsible for the September 11 [2001] attacks on the United States, reportedly has operation in 68 countries, from the Philippines and Indonesia to Egypt and Algeria. How many of those countries should be targeted for nation building? And al-Qaeda isn't the only terrorist organization out there. According to the State Department's latest *Patterns of Global Terrorism*, there are 42 other significant terrorist organizations operating in dozens of countries around the globe. Complicating matters still further—at least under [former U.N. Secretary General Kofi] Annan's sprawling definition of potential terrorist threats—are an estimated 106 countries with oppressive or semioppressive governments. That means as many as 3.6 billion people, or 59 percent of the world's population, should logically become the subjects of foreign nation-building efforts. Such numbers raise obvious practical questions.

Furthermore, the idea that "Nation Building Is the Best Defense" rests on several debatable assumptions—such as that poverty and ignorance are the "root causes" of terrorism and that undertaking multiple nation-building missions will significantly reduce the potential for terrorist acts. . . .

Do Poverty and Ignorance Cause Terrorism?

Hardly a day goes by without a politician or expert proposing more foreign aid or support for education as a cure for terrorism. "The dragon's teeth are planted in the fertile soil of . . . poverty and deprivation," [former] British prime minister Tony Blair tells us, so foreign assistance efforts must be ramped up around the world because that will reduce the terrorist threat. Jessica Stern, a Harvard University lecturer on terrorism, proclaims, "We have a stake in the welfare of other peoples and need to devote a much higher priority to health, education, and economic development, or new Osamas will continue to arise." Her clear implication: If these issues are adequately addressed, the terrorist threat will be reduced or eliminated.

That line of reasoning, however, makes several false assumptions about the root causes of terrorism. For starters, no evidence links poverty and ignorance to the present terrorist challenge faced by the United States. Bin Laden is a multimillionaire, and the hijackers who flew fully fueled jetliners into the World Trade Center and the Pentagon on September 11 [2001] were highly educated and well off. Bin Laden, moreover, has never claimed that he acts on behalf of the poor and the illiterate, or that his goal is to redress the disparities between rich and poor countries. His goal is to eliminate opposition and gain power.

The "root causes" explanation is flawed for another reason: Poverty can exist without terrorism, as it did during the Great Depression and does . . . in most of sub-Saharan Africa. And terrorism can thrive without poverty. In fact, left-wing terrorists, such as the German Baader-Meinhoff gang and the Italian Red Brigade, during the 1970s and 1980s were overwhelmingly middle class, and 15 of the 19 September 11 hijackers were from Saudi Arabia, an exceptionally rich country. If the view that poverty and ignorance cause terrorism were correct, then Saudis would be some of the most peaceful people on earth. Instead, Saudi Arabia is a top breeding ground for terrorists. In fact, a recent survey of educated Saudis between the ages of 25 and 41 found that 95 percent of them "had sympathy for the cause of . . . Osama bin Laden."

The Myth of the Uneducated Terrorist

Moreover, if there were any truth to the idea that poverty and ignorance are the root causes of terrorism, one would also expect terrorism to rise in countries during periods of economic hardship and fall during boom times. "In fact, the opposite tends to hold," says Alan Krueger, professor of economics and public affairs at Princeton University. The academic evidence on terrorists "suggests that the common stereotype that they come from the ranks of the most uneducated and economically deprived is a myth." Indeed, consider the research of United Nations relief worker Nasra Hassan. From 1996 to 1999 she interviewed nearly 250 people involved in terrorist attacks, including failed bombers, families of deceased bombers, and trainers. Her conclusion, as reported by Krueger. "None of them were uneducated, desperately poor, simpleminded, or depressed."

Professor Ariel Merari, director of the Political Violence Research Center at Tel Aviv University, agrees: "All information that I have also indicates that there is no connection between socioeconomic indicators and involvement in militant/terrorist activity in general and in suicide attacks in particular, at least as much as the Palestinian case is concerned."

Similarly, Egyptian social scientist Saad Eddin Ibrahim has found that followers of militant Islam in his country tend not to be children of poverty and ignorance. After interviewing several of them serving time in Egytian prisons, he discovered that the typical member is "young (early twenties), of rural or small-town background, from the middle or lower-middle class, with high achievement and motivation, upwardly mobile, with science or engineering education, and from a normally cohesive family." In short, Ibrahim found that these individuals were "significantly above average in their generation" and otherwise "ideal or model young Egyptians." In a subsequent study, he found that 21 of 34 members of the militant At-Takfir w'al-Hijra group in Egypt had fathers who were not impoverished; they were midlevel bureaucrats. More recently, the Canadian Security Intelligence Service noted that the leadership of another militant Egyptian group, Al-Jihad, "is largely university educated with middle-class backgounds." . . .

Failure in the Global Economy

The "root causes" approach also wrongly assumes that the United States and its allies are in a position to alleviate poverty and ignorance around the globe. The source of poverty and ignorance in much of the world tends to lie in the unwillingness of many states—especially in the Muslim world—to make themselves competitive in the global economy. Poor countries, in other words, have adopted poor policies. The key to becoming rich does not lie in another splurge of foreign aid. It lies in poor countries adopting policies that reduce trade barriers, respect the rule of law and private property, curb inflation, cut wasteful spending and corruption, and limit meddling in domestic markets. Western governments can augment those reforms by opening their own markets to Third World exports. [As of 2002], the United States imposes its highest trade barriers on the exports that are most important to poor countries, such as sugar, footwear, clothing, and textiles. Washington could deliver far more immediate and long-lasting "aid" to poor farmers and workers around the world by allowing them to sell what they produce duty-free in the U.S. market. But the bulk of the necessary reforms must be made by the countries themselves. . . .

Failed States and Old Borders

When it comes to combating terrorism in lands where there is no government to deter—that is, in failed states—recommending the nation-building solution misconstrues the *political* problem. The problem of failed states is not usually one of too little outside involvement or not enough foreign aid. It is a problem of fake countries and flawed borders, which are usually the remnant of colonialism or the practical consequence of intercommunal warfare, or both. Redrawing new

boundaries has been anathema to policymakers, but it is the adherence to unrealistic old borders that creates failed states and their deadly byproducts.

Combating terrorism in failed states by nation building also misconstrues the *military* problem. Take Somalia, where U.S. forces were involved in nation building a decade ago. [Former] Deputy Secretary of Defense Paul Wolfowitz correctly notes that Somalia is a "special case because it really isn't a governed country at all. It also means there's not much to protect the terrorists when they get there." Jonathan Stevenson, a research fellow at the International Institute for Strategic Studies in London, agrees: "Keeping al-Qaeda out of Somalia—not pacifying the country—is the prime objective. This . . . will not require a commitment of the 25,000 ground troops deployed in 1992–93, and will not raise comparable force-protection concerns." In other words, if the goal is to combat terrorism, then nation building in failed states is unwarranted. Failed states are where the terrorists are most vulnerable to covert action, commando raids, surprise attacks, and local informants willing to work for a few dollars. Failed states are not "safe havens"; they are defenseless positions.

Somali Warlords Play the Game

Appealing to the "Nation Building Is the Best Defense" lobby, however, three Somali warlords [in 2002] are calling for a new international military and political intervention in Somalia to rout out terrorism. But diplomats warn that the three warlords—including the one whose militia was responsible for the deaths of 18 U.S. Army Rangers in 1993 [son of warlord Mohammed Farrah Aidid]—have seized on the U.S. anti-terror campaign as their own route back to power. They apparently hope that accusing Somalia's shaky transitional national government of doing too little to combat terrorism will convince Washington to intervene and destroy the transitional government on their behalf. According to one official familiar with Somalia, "The new game in town is to call your enemy a terrorist and hope that America will destroy him for you."

There are already signs that this phenomenon is occurring in Afghanistan. In December 2001 U.S. air strikes destroyed a convoy on a road in Paktia province. The Pentagon said the attack was a legitimate and deliberate strike on fleeing Taliban officials, but Afghan leaders protested that it was a mistake, that the convoy was made up of local leaders on their way to Kabul for the inauguration of Afghanistan's new leader, Hamid Karzai. Both sides were partially correct. The convoy was made up of tribal elders heading to Kabul, and they were Taliban who had just switched sides when it became clear to them that the United States was going to win the war. An informant, who did not like someone in the convoy, told U.S. military operatives the convoy was Taliban, so U.S. warplanes destroyed the convoy, killing more than 50 people.

According to an Afghan intelligence officer, feuding Afghan clans have also been using the hunt for bin Laden and

Taliban chief Mullah Mohammad Omar to mislead U.S. forces and drag them into Afghanistan's age-old tribal disputes. In January 2002 American special forces raided Hazar Qadam, 60 miles north of Kandahar [in southern Afghanistan]. Local villagers claimed that U.S. troops were badly misled about the operation, which they say killed 15 anti-Taliban fighters headed by Haji Sana Gul, a local ethnic leader who had just disarmed a number of Taliban soldiers still holding out in the area. A U.S. Army spokesman said that suggestions that anti-Taliban forces had been wrongly attacked "are not consistent with our intelligence." But American officials have since acknowledged that they made a mistake and admitted they rely on information from members of rival ethnic groups whose loyalties are frequently shifting. . . .

Too Much Intervention

But why should outside "engagement" have been the default U.S. position after Washington helped Afghanistan to liberate itself? That France did not stick around to nation build in the United States after it helped the American colonists throw off the British crown was a good thing. What's more, Afghanistan had been relatively stable from 1930 through 1978. The reality is that it was external meddling—not the lack of it—that disrupted internal Afghan politics and led to the emergence of the Taliban. First, the Soviet-backed Afghan communists sought to impose their authoritarian rule on a fiercely independent and traditional society. That led to civil war [from 1979 to 1989]. Then the United States further unbalanced Afghanistan's internal politics by supporting its most extreme anti-Soviet and anti-modern elements. Finally, Pakistan's internal security services, or ISI, supported the Taliban faction, because it was best positioned to secure Islamabad's [Pakistan's capital] strategic interests in the region. The lesson of Afghanistan is not that there hasn't been enough outside meddling but that there has been too much.

VIEWPOINT

> "The Bush administration [realizes] that helping certain states rebuild is indeed in the U.S. strategic interest, lest these same states once again give rise to the sort of regimes that allow the al Qaedas of this world to thrive within their borders."

Nation-Building Can Defeat Terrorism

Mark Burgess

Mark Burgess is a research assistant at the Center for Defense Information (CDI). In this viewpoint, Burgess argues that perceived failure by the United States and United Nations in Somalia created an American political fear of nation-building. Somalia, he writes, was not disastrous as a humanitarian operation, and could have progressed to nation-building if the U.S. military had understood that combat against terrorists and nation-building are part of the same mission. Equating the two in the future, he argues, will allow the United States to fight terrorism and succeed as humanitarians.

Mark Burgess, "A Natural Fear Increased with Tales: America's Aversion to Nation-Building and Peacekeeping," *CDI Terrorism Project*, March 8, 2002. www.cdi.org. Reproduced by permission.

As you read, consider the following questions:

1. According to the author, what did the outcome of the U.S. mission in Somalia, despite its failures, finally reveal?
2. Why is keeping the peace in Afghanistan linked to fighting a war there, according to Burgess?
3. If America is to operate in complex, failed state emergencies, fear of what must be overcome, according to the viewpoint author?

President George W. Bush has long been critical of American involvement in peacekeeping missions generally, arguing since the 2000 presidential election campaign that commitment to such operations over-extends the U.S. military and should be reassessed. This stance has, if anything, become more intractable since the current military campaign against terrorism began, as evidenced by the recent announcement of the intent to scale back the U.S. commitment to the Multinational Force and Observers in Sinai [Egyptian peninsula between the Mediterranean and Red seas]. Similarly, while meeting with [Afghanistan leader Hamid] Karzai in Washington on Jan. 28 [2002], Bush pledged $50 million in aid and undertook to assist Afghanistan in establishing a national army and police force, but insisted that U.S. troops would not take part in any long-term peacekeeping force in the country. This opposition to peacekeeping is further evidenced by the reluctance of some within the U.S. administration to endorse calls for ISAF's [International Security Assistance Force] expansion.

Misreading Somalia

Partly, America's aversion to peacekeeping can be traced back to the ill-fated operation in Somalia [1993 to 1995]. This ended after the death of 18 U.S. military personnel, and resulted in a marked loss of enthusiasm for peace operations, as witnessed by the Clinton administration's release of Presidential Decision Directive 25. The prospect of another Somalia-type fiasco led to an aversion to nation building, and has been cited by some, such as [former] Sen. Jesse Helms, R-N.C. [in 2002], as a sufficient rationale for America not to get involved in peacekeeping in Afghanistan.

However, as one former American UN official in Mogadishu says of the operation in Somalia: "The mission was not fated to fail. It failed because of UN and U.S. bungling." Arguably, the Somalia operation did not succeed because it vacillated between the extremes of too much or too little force, finally overstretching itself in the ill-advised and ill-fated manhunt for the Somali warlord Mohammed Aideed. This amounted to a declaration of war against Aideed, and was a step too far. The mission ended in failure, a casualty of applying too much force with too little regard for the consequences.

This contrasted with the success enjoyed by the U.S. Marines of the Unified Taskforce (UNITAF) that had been previously deployed in Somalia. UNITAF enjoyed considerable success in fulfilling its mandate "to establish a secure environment for humanitarian relief operations," and allowed the United Nations and various non-governmental organizations in Somalia to operate in relative safety and counter the worst effects of the countrywide famine within months. Furthermore, "though postured for enforcement, it [UNITAF] behaved in many ways like a peacekeeping contingent, and it did so in an environment where each of the parties was ultrasensitive to any hint of bias against its interests." As such, the UNITAF operation, while not full-blown nation building, was certainly more worthy of the name than the armed posse that went after Aideed. Moreover, it not only went some way towards proving that the concept of nation building was achievable, but demonstrated that peacekeeping in the post-Cold War "New World Order" was also doable, albeit with great difficulty. Similarly, the success of operations in Mozambique and

Spreading the Ink

One point missing from the discussion about the linkages between security and development so far has been mention of the ink spot strategy. Employed successfully by the British in Malaya fifty years ago and given more recent prominence by the former army officer and American academic Andrew Krepinevich, it involves focusing military effort not on hunting down the enemy, but instead securing key centers and improving conditions there so markedly that you eliminate support for an insurgency. Success then spreads slowly outwards as if from an expanding ink spot (hence the designation).

In Afghanistan, the importance of filling those "ungoverned spaces" where the Taliban has been undergoing a revival has been promoted by General David Richards, the British Commander of the current 36-nation NATO-led International Security Assistance Force (ISAF)....

In essence, the ink spot strategy might best be explained as being akin to expanding Kabul's Green Zone—known in more politically correct terminology as the International Zone—outwards to the entire country, where the benefits of the international presence, security, spending and government are visible and obvious for all.

Greg Mills and Terrence McNamee,
"Security Vortex, Warlords and Nation Building,"
National Interest *online, September 1, 2006.*
www.nationalinterest.org.

Uganda testify that helping devastated countries rebuild need not end as ignobly as did the American adventure in Somalia.

Scrapping Peacekeeping

Such examples provide a strong counter-balance to the argument that nation building is to be avoided at all costs. To a degree, this position has changed since Sept. 11, with the Bush administration realizing that helping certain states rebuild is indeed in the U.S. strategic interest, lest these same states once again give rise to the sort of regimes that allow the al Qaedas of this world to thrive within their borders. However, true nation building has been replaced by what has been termed "nation building lite." This differs from both the concentrated nation building that took place in former Axis countries following the Second World War, and that which occurred in the Third World in the post-colonial period. Instead, the focus is on assisting failed states train new armies and police forces and rebuild their governmental and economic institutions.

Nation building lite also appears to eschew peacekeeping as shown by [former] U.S. Defense Secretary Donald Rumsfeld's remarks when asked about expanding ISAF: "Another school of thought, which is where my brain is, is that why put all the time and money and effort in that? Why not put it into helping them develop a national army, so that they can look out for themselves over time?" Such an outcome would be desirable.

However, a monopoly on the legitimate use of force remains a prerequisite of modern statehood. The government of Afghanistan does not, as yet, possess such a monopoly and may require outside assistance if it is to survive long enough to acquire it. The expansion of ISAF would provide just such assistance, buying enough time for the Afghan government to build up the national army rightly referred to by Rumsfeld as being so necessary.

A Crucial Link: Politics and War

The paradoxical nature of America's policy towards peacekeeping in Afghanistan is further evidenced by the comments of Douglas J. Feith, the [former] U.S. undersecretary of defense for policy [from 2001 to 2005]. Feith contends: "We do have an interest in the kind of stability in Afghanistan that will make it less likely that Afghanistan will become a base for terrorist operations against us in the future. We want the current Afghan political experiment to succeed." However, this conflicts with his added qualifier: "We are not involving ourselves in internecine politics, including the politics backed by guns, as the definition of our military mission." Such proclamations are dangerously dismissive of the crucial link between politics and war.

For, distasteful and inconvenient though it may be, keeping the peace in Afghanistan is inextricably linked to fighting a war there. Not only will this help prevent the reemergence of the conditions which gave rise to al Qaeda's biggest ally, it will also guard against America's acquiring a reputation as a global bully who cares little for picking up the pieces after its devastating military campaigns. Leaving aside any moral imperative attached to assisting Afghanistan through its present difficulties, the propaganda coup handed to America's enemies by any failure to do so is surely sufficient argument for such assistance. Given this, any contentions that ISAF's expansion presents an unnecessary diversion of resources from the larger war effort against terrorism are debatable. In the current strategic climate, warfighting and peacekeeping are two sides of one coin. Indeed, given the previously mentioned continuity in the negative U.S. attitude towards peacekeeping generally, such protestations of over-commitment almost seem like mere justification of existing policy—especially in light of the sheer scale of the recently announced defense budget.

Mission Creep

Fear of "mission creep" may also play a part in such opposition. Such prudence is wise. As [former U.S. ambassador to Somalia] Robert B. Oakley says of the unfolding situation in Afghanistan [as of 2002]: "It's difficult, it's tricky and you've got to be very, very careful not to get in too deep and say, 'We're king makers.'" However, as Oakley adds, the United

States still needs to accept that it is already involved in Afghanistan's affairs, and has sided with the interim authority [of Hamid Karzai]. As such, it needs to support this authority to the fullest extent while also remaining sensitive to regional opinion. Oakley's comments are noteworthy, not least because, as a former U.S. ambassador to Somalia, he speaks with some authority on the issue.

These remarks also allude to how fine the line between prudence and vacillation can be when a clearly defined exit strategy becomes a non-negotiable prerequisite to initiating urgently needed military action. The U.S. tendency toward such practices, as evident in the run-up to operations in the Persian Gulf, the Balkans, and the present campaign in Afghanistan, caused one commentator to note recently: "The modesty of our [America's] aims in entering wars is surpassed only by the timidity with which we conclude them." This is not to say that such tendencies are uniquely American, as events in the United Kingdom show, with opposition members of parliament charging that the British government has committed troops to ISAF without considering how they will be withdrawn. Nor should military operations be undertaken without proper regard to how they will end—as the Vietnam War graphically demonstrated. However, the desire for neat exit strategies must guide the parameters of such operations, not dictate them. Indeed, friction in war, as identified by [Prussian military officer Carl Phillipp von] Clausewitz [who wrote the influential book *On War*] ensures such strategies are not always achievable even when they exist.

As such, fears over mission creep must be kept in perspective. Otherwise, America will not find itself creeping into missions as much as being dragged in, something that may yet prove the case in Afghanistan should ISAF not be expanded. Indeed, to a degree this is already happening, with U.S. troops engaged in humanitarian operations even as their comrades engage in the heaviest ground combat of the war to date.

There have also been charges that the U.S. may have already intervened (perhaps even inadvertently) with air strikes in factional fighting in Afghanistan. As such factors further illustrate, if America is to adequately operate in the gray zone of complex emergencies, the fear of mission creep must be overcome, along with the larger U.S. aversion to peacekeeping and nation building of which it is part. Looming large in sustaining this aversion is the specter of Somalia. Like the ghosts of Vietnam before it, this must be exorcised if the United States is to effectively meet the challenge of twenty-first century warfare.

> *"We cannot impose democracy in Iraq any more than we can erase hundreds of years of Iraqi history."*

Nation-Building Cannot Defeat Terrorism, Part I

Ron Paul

Ron Paul argues in this viewpoint that American global nation-building is best expressed by the failures of the Iraq occupation and the U.S. failure to understand the ethnic, historical climate of the country. He believes the United States should return to the conservative, noninterventionist strategies of the Founding Fathers before we completely alienate the Islamic world and elevate support for terrorists. Ron Paul is a Republican congressman from Texas who is running for president in 2008.

As you read, consider the following questions:

1. According to Paul, what happens when the U.S. goes to war without a Congressional declaration of war?

2. What is creating the conditions for civil war in Iraq, according to the viewpoint author?

Ron Paul, "Nation-Building Is Not Conservative," *anti-war.com*, December 14, 2004. www.anti-war.com. Reproduced by permission.

3. America's founding fathers could not have imagined the modern world when they wrote the Constitution. Does this justify nation-building abroad, according to Paul?

A [2004] study by the Pentagon's Defense Science Task Force on Strategic Communications concluded that in the struggle for hearts and minds in Iraq, "American efforts have not only failed, they may also have achieved the opposite of what they intended." This Pentagon report flatly states that our war in Iraq actually has elevated support for radical Islamists. It goes on to conclude that our active intervention in the Middle East as a whole has greatly diminished our reputation in the region, and strengthened support for radical groups. This is similar to what the CIA predicted in an October 2002 National Intelligence Estimate, before the invasion took place.

Then, [in December 2004] we learned that the CIA station chief in Baghdad sent a cable back to the U.S. warning that the situation in Iraq is deteriorating, and not expected to improve any time soon. Other CIA experts also warn that the security situation in Iraq is likely to get even worse in the future. These reports are utterly ignored by the [President George W. Bush] administration.

A Folly of Nation-Building

These recent reports are not the product of some radical antiwar organization. They represent the U.S. government's own assessment of our "progress" in Iraq [as of 2004] and the loss of thousands of lives. We are alienating the Islamic world in our oxymoronic quest to impose democracy in Iraq.

This demonstrates once again the folly of nation-building, which is something candidate [George W.] Bush wisely rejected before the 2000 election. The worsening situation in Iraq also reminds us that going to war without a congressional declaration, as the Constitution requires, leads us into protracted quagmires over and over again.

Money Can't Buy Security

If preventing terrorism and conflict was simply a matter of financial grants to unstable or troubled regions, then U.S. aid to Palestinians would have paved the road map to peace, and India's half-century long financial subsidies to Jammu and Kashmir would have prevented that state from becoming a nuclear flashpoint. Similarly, Soviet attempts at nation-building in Afghanistan in the 1980s should have led to popular support for that occupation.

Subodh Atal,
"Nation-Building Secures Neither Homeland Nor the World,"
The Cato Institute, November 24, 2003. www.cato.org.

Creating an Iraqi Civil War

The reality is that current-day Iraq contains three distinct groups of people who have been at odds with each other for generations. Pundits and politicians tell us that a civil war will erupt if the U.S. military departs. Yet our insistence that Iraq remain one indivisible nation actually creates the conditions for civil war. Instead of an artificial, forced, nationalist unity between the Sunnis, Shi'ites, and Kurds, we should allow each group to seek self-government and choose voluntarily whether they wish to associate with a central government. We cannot impose democracy in Iraq any more than we can erase hundreds of years of Iraqi history.

Even opponents of the war now argue that we must occupy Iraq indefinitely until a democratic government takes hold, no matter what the costs. No attempt is made by either side to explain exactly why it is the duty of American soldiers to die for the benefit of Iraq or any other foreign country. No reason is given why American taxpayers must pay billions of dollars to build infrastructure in Iraq. We are expected to accept the interventionist approach without question, as though no other options exist. This blanket acceptance of foreign meddling and foreign aid may be the current Republican policy, but it is not a conservative policy by any means.

Misusing the Constitution

Non-interventionism was the foreign policy ideal of the Founding Fathers, an ideal that is ignored by both political parties today. Those who support political and military intervention in Iraq and elsewhere should have the integrity to admit that their views conflict with the principles of our nation's founding. It's easy to repeat the tired cliché that "times have changed since the Constitution was written"—in fact, that's an argument the left has used for decades to justify an unconstitutional welfare state. Yet if we accept this argument, what other principles from the founding era should we discard? Should we reject federalism? Habeas corpus [court order allowing detainees to seek legal relief from unlawful jailing]? How about the Second Amendment [the right to bear arms]? The principle of limited government enshrined in the Constitution—limited government in both domestic and foreign affairs—has not changed over time. What has changed is our willingness to ignore that principle.

> *"The longer and more extensive the occupation of Muslim territories, the greater the chance of more 9/11-type attacks on the U.S."*

Nation-Building Cannot Defeat Terrorism, Part II

Ron Paul

In this viewpoint, Ron Paul argues that if we are to stop the spread of suicide bombers (for instance, the September 11, 2001 plane highjackers), we must understand the reasons suicide bombers carry out their terrorist attacks. Paul has come to believe that U.S. intervention and nation-building abroad foster and promote a suicide ideology, making America more vulnerable to terrorists and suicide combat. Ron Paul is a U.S. congressman from Texas. He is running for President in 2008.

As you read, consider the following questions:

1. Why did many Americans initially support the war and occupation of Iraq, according to Paul?

2. How important are religious beliefs to suicide bombers, according to the viewpoint author?

Ron Paul, "Ending Suicide Terrorism," *anti-war.com*, July 21, 2005. www.antiwar .com. Reproduced by permission.

3. Paul believes there is a solution, that does not involve nation-building, to halting suicide bombing. What is it?

More than half of the American people [as of 2005] believe that the Iraqi war [the occupation of Iraq by the United States since 2003] has made the U.S. less safe. This is a dramatic shift in sentiment from two years ago. Early support for the war reflected a hope for a safer America, and it was thought to be an appropriate response to the 9/11 attacks. The argument was that the enemy attacked us because of our freedom, our prosperity, and our way of life. It was further argued that it was important to engage the potential terrorists over there rather than here. Many bought this argument and supported the war. That is now changing.

It is virtually impossible to stop determined suicide bombers. Understanding why they sacrifice themselves is crucial to ending what appears to be senseless and irrational. But there is an explanation.

Rethinking Terrorism

I, like many, have assumed that the driving force behind the suicide attacks was Islamic fundamentalism. Promise of instant entry into paradise as a reward for killing infidels seemed to explain the suicides, a concept that is foreign to our way of thinking. The world's expert on suicide terrorism has convinced me to rethink this simplistic explanation, that terrorism is merely an expression of religious extremism and resentment of a foreign culture.

Robert Pape, author of *Dying to Win*, explains the strategic logic of suicide terrorism. Pape has collected a database of every suicide terrorist attack between 1980 and 2004, all 462 of them. His conclusions are enlightening and crucial to our understanding the true motivation behind the attacks against Western nations by Islamic terrorists. After his exhaustive study, Pape comes to some very important conclusions.

Nations Aren't Military Products

Is the military really cut out to build a private sector? It takes a rather shallow knowledge of history not to know that private sectors are not built; they evolve. They certainly are not the product of precision bombs and bayonets. Just as ludicrous is the idea that the military will "develop representative governmental institutions."

Sheldon Richman, "Nation-Building Is Now Job One,"
The Future of Freedom Foundation, December 21, 2005. www.fff.org.

Misreading Religious Beliefs

Religious beliefs are less important than supposed. For instance, the Tamil Tigers in Sri Lanka, a Marxist secular group, are the world's leader in suicide terrorism. The largest Islamic fundamentalist countries have not been responsible for any suicide terrorist attack. None have come from Iran or the Sudan. Until the U.S. invasion of Iraq, Iraq never had a suicide terrorist attack in all of its history. Between 1995 and 2004, the al-Qaeda [the international terrorist group led by Osama bin Laden] years, two-thirds of all attacks came from countries where the U.S. had troops stationed. Iraq's suicide missions today are carried out by Iraqi Sunnis and Saudis. Recall, 15 of the 19 participants in the 9/11 attacks were Saudis.

The clincher is this: the strongest motivation, according to Pape, is not religion but rather a desire "to compel modern democracies to withdraw military forces from the territory the terrorists view as their homeland."

A Solution to Suicide Bombing

The best news is that if stopping suicide terrorism is a goal we seek, a solution is available to us. Cease the occupation of foreign lands, and the suicide missions will cease. Between 1982 and 1986, there were 41 suicide terrorist attacks in Lebanon. Once the U.S., the French, and Israel withdrew their forces from Lebanon, there were no more attacks. The reason the attacks stop, according to Pape, is that the Osama bin Ladens of the world no longer can inspire potential suicide terrorists despite their continued fanatical religious beliefs.

Pape is convinced after his extensive research that the longer and more extensive the occupation of Muslim territories, the greater the chance of more 9/11-type attacks on the U.S. He is convinced that the terrorists strategically are holding off hitting the U.S. at the present time in an effort to break up the coalition by hitting our European allies. He claims it is just a matter of time if our policies do not change.

It is time for us to consider a strategic reassessment of our policy of foreign interventionism, occupation, and nation-building. It is in our national interest and in the interest of world peace to do so.

Periodical Bibliography

The following articles have been selected to supplement the diverse views presented in this chapter.

Robert C. Byrd   "Regain the Focus on the War on Terrorism," *U.S. Senator Robert C. Byrd speech*, September 10, 2003, http://byrd.senate.gov.

Ted Galen Carpenter   "The Imperial Lure: Nation-Building as a US Response to Terrorism," *The Mediterranean Quarterly*, Winter 2006.

Kenneth D. Comfort   "Preventing Terrorism Through Nation-Building: A Viable Way?" U.S. Army War College, July 4, 2003, www.au.af.mil.

Council for Foreign Relations   "Terrorism Havens: Lebanon," Background Paper, July 2006, www.cfr.org.

James Dobbins   "Nation-Building Returns to Favour," The Rand Corporation, August 11, 2004, www.rand.org.

Stuart E. Eizenstadt   "Rebuilding Weak States," *Foreign Affairs*, January/February 2005.

M. Ashraf Haidari   "How Goes the War (on Terrorism)? Nation-Building or Nation-Neglecting?" *SFGate.com, San Francisco Chronicle*, February 6, 2007, www.sfgate.com.

Naomi Klein   "The Rise of Disaster Capitalism," *Nation*, May 2, 2005, www.nation.com.

Stephen Leahy   "Bungled Peace-Building Opens Door to Terrorism," Inter Press Service News Agency, February 1, 2006, www.ipsnews.net.

Alan Sorenson   "The Reluctant Nation Builders," *Current History*, December 2003.

Ramesh Thakur   "The War on Terrorism and the United Nations," United Nations University, 2003, www.unu.edu.

CHAPTER 3

Can Nation-Building in Iraq Work?

Chapter Preface

Analysts of President George W. Bush administration's mission in Iraq, begun with the 2003 invasion, sometimes note similarities between the Iraq occupation and the American war in Vietnam (1959–1975). The American escalation in Vietnam brought soldiers and nation-building specialists. Nation-building was called by many names: Rural Pacification, Vietnamization, Civil Operations and Revolutionary Development (CORDS), and others.

The United States believed that it could clear Communist elements out of villages, hamlets, and cities. The South Vietnamese Army would be trained, funded, and supervised by the Americans. They would take control of securing the areas the Americans had cleared. The American response to the Iraq insurgency has been similar. The American military is again attempting to train an indigenous force that is competing with various private militias, so that it can police and fight insurgents.

As of this writing, analysts and politicians continue to haggle over the best method for an American military withdrawal out of Iraq, in what has become an unpopular war with the American public, just as the Vietnam War lost public support.

Truong Tran served in the South Vietnamese Army from 1964 to 1969, fighting against the Communist Viet Cong. Badly wounded in a 1967 battle, he went to work with American nonprofit group Save the Children (STC) in South Vietnam. Tran administered nation-building at the lowest levels of South Vietnamese society. Poor families who needed economic assistance were given interest-free loans through STC. They repaid the loan into a communal redevelopment fund that funded other communal projects in their own villages. In 1971, he went to work for the U.S. State Department and the

CORDS program, which was attempting to accelerate rebuilding and modernization in the South Vietnamese countryside. However, Tran came to realize that corruption was endemic to the process. The U.S. State Department gave money to provincial leaders for specific local projects, but little of it made it to the village level.

The biggest problem Tran observed, though, was the chaotic infusion of U.S. military culture into South Vietnam. Recalling those years in Christian G. Appy's book *Patriots: The Vietnam War Remembered from All Sides*, Tran recounts:

> Having U.S. soldiers in Vietnam not only destroyed our political cause, it also destroyed our economy and social fabric. Ninety percent of the population had relied on the land, but during the war people could not grow crops and had to move to the cities. Some people were lucky enough to get jobs with U.S. military, but many had to become menial laborers or even prostitutes. . . . To support their families many people abused their power to make more money. Of course there was corruption, but how could you live on twenty dollars and maintain the will to fight?

The U.S. withdrawal from Vietnam, though popular with the antiwar movement in America, collapsed the nation-building programs the United States had instituted. The North Vietnamese military quickly seized South Vietnam, unifying the country under the control of the Communist North's government. Vietnamese allies of the Americans were executed, tortured, and imprisoned at the infamous Communist "reeducation camps," where hard labor and physical abuse were the norm.

The United States once again confronts nation-building after its armed intervention in a foreign country deemed strategically significant to its national security. There is, arguably, a civil war being fought amongst Iraqis alongside U.S. attempts to stabilize the situation, reconstruct the country, and promote democracy. If the United States hastily withdrew from Iraq, as it ultimately did in South Vietnam, could nation-building ever succeed there? This is one of the many questions the authors of the following viewpoints face as they seek, in opposing arguments, to answer the chapter's title question.

> *"We are not in Iraq to engage in nation-building—our mission is to help Iraqis so that they can build their own nation."*

U.S. Nation-Building in Iraq Will Work

Donald H. Rumsfeld

Donald H. Rumsfeld was the U. S. secretary of defense from 2000 to 2006. He led the Defense Department as part of President George W. Bush's response to the September 11, 2001 terrorist attacks, and the invasion and reconstruction efforts in Afghanistan and Iraq. Rumsfeld argues in this viewpoint that nation-building in both countries will succeed because the United States is prepared to use a new model of nation-building, one that aids the Iraqis and Afghans in rebuilding their own countries rather than dictating the reconstruction agenda.

As you read, consider the following questions:

1. Why did the media predict failure at the beginning of the war against Iraq, and at the beginning of nation-building after the war, according to Rumsfeld?

2. According to Rumsfeld, will long-term stability in Iraq come from the presence of foreign aid workers?

Donald H. Rumsfeld, "Beyond Nation-Building," *Washington Post*, September 25, 2003, p. A33. www.washingtonpost.com.

3. Does the biggest threat to Iraqi peace and nation-building come from terrorists and former dictator Saddam Hussein's friends, according to the viewpoint author?

Two weeks into Operation Iraqi Freedom [the invasion of Iraq, begun March 20, 2003], a number of newspapers and many airwaves were filled with prognosticators declaring the war plan a failure. The United States, they said, did not do enough to build international support, did not properly anticipate the level of resistance by Iraqis, and failed to send enough forces to do the job.

Then coalition forces took Baghdad in 21 days. Today [General] Tom Franks's [commanding general of the U.S. invasion of Iraq] innovative and flexible war plan, which so many dismissed as a failure, is being studied by military historians and taught in war colleges.

An Innovative Postwar Plan

Today in Iraq [September 2003], an innovative plan is also being implemented in our effort to win the peace. And it should come as no surprise that we are again hearing suggestions as to why the postwar effort is on the brink of failure.

It will take longer than 21 days, but I believe that the plan to win the peace in Iraq will succeed—just as the plan to win the war succeeded.

Why did some predict failure in the first weeks of the war? One reason, I suspect, is that Gen. Franks's plan was different and unfamiliar—in short, not what was expected. And because it didn't fit into the template of general expectations, many assumed at the first setback that the underlying strategy had to be flawed. It wasn't. Setbacks were expected, and the plan was designed to be flexible so our forces could deal with surprise. The coalition forces did so exceedingly well.

A New Kind of Nation-Building

I believe the same will be true of the effort in Iraq today. Once again, what the coalition is doing is unfamiliar and different from many past "nation-building" efforts. So, when the coalition faces the inevitable surprises and setbacks, the assumption is that the underlying strategy is failing. I do not believe that is the case. To the contrary, despite real dangers, I believe that the new approach being taken by [General] John Abizaid [replaced Gen. Tommy Franks as commander-in-chief, American Occupation Forces, in May 2003] and Ambassador L. Paul Bremer [named by President George W. Bush as director of reconstruction and humanitarian assistance and head of the coalition provisional authority for postwar Iraq on May 6, 2003] will succeed and that success will have an important impact, not just on the future of Iraq but also on future international efforts to help struggling nations recover from war and regain self-reliance.

Today in Iraq we are operating on the same guiding principle that has brought success to our effort in Afghanistan: Iraq and Afghanistan belong to the Iraqi and Afghan peoples— the United States does not aspire to own or run those countries.

During the war in Afghanistan, this philosophy helped shape the military campaign. Instead of sending a massive invasion force, we kept the coalition footprint modest and adopted a strategy of teaming with local Afghan forces that opposed the Taliban. The use of precision-guided weapons and the immediate delivery of humanitarian relief sent the message that we were coming as a force of liberation. And after the major fighting ended, we did not flood Afghanistan with Americans but rather worked with Afghans to establish an interim government and an Afghan national army. In Iraq the military challenge was notably different. No force of Iraqi fighters could have toppled the Saddam Hussein regime without significant numbers of coalition forces—though in the north, Special Operations forces and Kurdish *pesh merga* [Kurdish militia] fighters did tie down Hussein's northern units and liberate Mosul. Even so, we did not flood the country with a half-million U.S. troops. We kept our footprint modest, liberating Iraq with a little more than 100,000 U.S. troops on the ground. The use of precision weapons allowed us to save innocent lives and make clear that this was a war against a regime, not a people. And when major combat operations ended, we began working immediately to enlist Iraqis to take responsibility for governance and security.

Postwar Progress

We have made solid progress: Within two months, all major Iraqi cities and most towns had municipal councils—something that took eight months in postwar Germany. Within four months the Iraqi Governing Council had appointed a cabinet—something that took 14 months in Germany. An independent Iraqi Central Bank was established and a new currency announced in just two months—accomplishments that took three years in postwar Germany. Within two months a new Iraqi police force was conducting joint patrols with coalition forces. Within three months, we had begun training a new Iraqi army—and today some 56,000 are participating in the defense of their country. By contrast, it took 14 months to establish a police force in Germany and 10 years to begin training a new German army.

Why is enlisting Iraqis in security and governance so important?

Because it is their country. We are not in Iraq to engage in nation-building—our mission is to help Iraqis so that they can build their own nation. That is an important distinction.

A foreign presence in any country is unnatural. It is much like a broken bone. If it's not set properly at the outset, the muscles and tendons will grow around the break, and eventually the body will adjust to the abnormal condition. This is

Oversight from Within

So the first duty of any nation-builder, under conditions of occupation, is to recognize that it is exercising political power on behalf of the people whom it is governing. And in that capacity, it has to take responsibility for acting in their interests, just like any other democratic government. So the nation-builder has to allow for oversight by the people who live in the country—through allowing free speech, free assembly, and encouraging active participation through various consultative bodies.

Bradford Plummer,
"What We Owe Iraq: An Interview with Noah Feldman,"
Mother Jones, *January 16, 2005. www.motherjones.com.*

what has happened in some past nation-building exercises. Well-intentioned foreigners arrive on the scene, look at the problems, and say, "Let's go fix it for them." Despite the good intentions and efforts of the international workers, there can be unintended adverse side effects. Because when foreigners come in with solutions to local problems, it can create dependency. Economies can remain unreformed, distorted and dependent. In some instances, educated young people make more money as drivers for international workers than as doctors or civil servants.

Independence, Not Dependency

For example, East Timor is one of the poorest countries in Asia, yet the capital is now one of the most expensive cities in Asia. Local restaurants are out of reach for most Timorese and cater to international workers, who are paid 200 times the average local wage. At the city's main supermarket, prices are reportedly on par with those in London and New York.

Or take Kosovo [a province of Serbia under U.N. peace-keeping administration since 1999]. A driver shuttling international workers around the capital earns 10 times the salary of a university professor, and the U.N. administration pays its local staff between four and 10 times the salary of doctors and nurses. Four years after the war, the United Nations still runs Kosovo by executive fiat, issuing postage stamps, passports and driver's licenses. Decisions made by the local elected parliament are invalid without the signature of the U.N. administrator. And still, to this day, Kosovar ministers have U.N. overseers with the power to approve or disapprove their decisions.

Our objective is not to create dependency but to encourage Iraqi independence, by giving Iraqis increasing responsibility, over time, for the security and governance of their country. Because long-term stability comes not from the presence of foreign forces but from the development of functioning local institutions. The sooner Iraqis can take responsibility for their own affairs the sooner U.S. forces can come home.

That is why the coalition has been recruiting Iraqis to help defend Iraq, why municipal councils have been formed in 90 percent of the country and why the Iraqi Governing Council is taking charge of developing the 2004 budget and creating a process for the drafting of a new constitution, written by Iraqis, so that the Iraqi people can eventually choose their leaders in free elections—and we can achieve an orderly transfer of full sovereignty.

Coalition efforts in both Iraq and Afghanistan are bearing fruit.

Afghanistan is on the path to stability and self-government—transformed from a safe haven for terrorism to an important U.S. ally, not just in the war against terror but also in the larger struggle for freedom and moderation in the Muslim world.

The Threat to Iraqi Nation-Building

In Iraq the regime is gone, and Iraqis are stepping forward to take responsibility for their country. They are serving local, regional and national governing institutions, signing up to serve as police, border guards, soldiers and civil defense forces, starting businesses, creating jobs and building a new nation from the rubble of Saddam Hussein's tyranny.

This is not to underestimate the challenges in Iraq today. Terrorists and regime remnants want to roll back our successes and stop the Iraqi people's transition to democracy and self-government. We can expect they will continue to attack our successes, and the brave Iraqis who work with us, for some time. But coalition forces are dealing with the threat. And the security situation is improving.

Indeed, we may find that the biggest threat in Iraq comes not from terrorists and regime remnants but from the physical and psychological effects of three decades of Stalinist [after Joseph Stalin, Communist Soviet Union dictator from 1928 to 1953] oppression. But Iraq also has a number of advantages— oil wealth, water and an elaborate system of irrigation canals, vast wheat and barley fields, biblical sites and the potential for tourism, and an educated, urban population.

The Price to Rebuild Iraq

But to help Iraqis succeed, we must proceed with some humility. American forces can do many remarkable things, but they cannot provide permanent stability or create an Iraqi democracy. That will be up to the Iraqi people.

The work in Iraq is difficult, costly and dangerous. But it is worth the risks and the costs, because if the coalition succeeds, Iraqis will take hold of their country, develop the institutions of self-government and reclaim their nation's place as a responsible member of the international community. If we succeed, we will deal terrorism a powerful blow, because a democratic Iraq in the heart of the Middle East would be a defeat for the ideology of terror that is seeking to take control of that area of the world.

It will take patience, but if we are steadfast, Iraq can become a model for a successful transition from tyranny to democracy and self-reliance, and a friend and ally of the United States and the world's free and peace-loving nations. A few months ago, that statement would have seemed fanciful to many. Today, it is a goal within reach. But only if we help Iraqis build their nation, instead of trying to do it for them— and have the wisdom to know the difference.

> *"It's tempting to suggest that the Bush Administration is failing to provide Iraq with functioning, efficient, reliable public services because it doesn't be-lieve in functioning, efficient, reliable public services."*

U.S. Nation-Building in Iraq Won't Work

Hendrik Hertzberg

Hendrik Hertzberg is a staff writer for The New Yorker *magazine. In this viewpoint, Hertzberg argues because the Bush administration's conservative philosophy does not believe in funding public services and infrastructure at home, its efforts in Iraq will be underfunded, and more importantly, lack the moral core to guarantee the success of the nation-building operation. When Americans fully understand the administration's philosophical foundation they will rebel against it and nation-building in Iraq.*

As you read, consider the following questions:

1. According to Hertzberg, the American promise of a new Iraq is failing on the basis of unmet basic services. What are they?

2. What does the author see as the moral failure of the Bush administration in Iraq and at home?

3. Is there a connection between tax cuts for the rich, promoted by the Bush administration at home, and funding for Iraq abroad, according to Hertzberg?

The other day, the [*New York*] *Times* quoted one of that ever-helpful breed, a "senior administration official," as expressing surprise at the horrendous condition of Iraq's "infrastructure," even before the destruction brought about by the war and its aftermath. "From the outside it looked like Baghdad was a city that works," the senior official said. "It isn't."

The quintessential city that works (or, at least, has a cleverly cultivated reputation for being the city that works) is, of course, Chicago. The ward heelers [a worker for a local political boss] and aldermen [member of a municipal assembly or council] of that city understand (or, at least, are celebrated in song and story for understanding) that political power flows not from the barrel of a gun, and not even, necessarily, from the ballot box (whose contents can change in the counting), but from the ability to fix potholes. Garbage that gets collected, buses and trains that take people places, cops that whack bad guys upside the head, taps that yield water when you turn them, lights that go on when you flip the switch, all lubricated by taxes and a bit of honest graft—these are what keep streets calm, voters pacified, and righteous "reformers" out of City Hall.

A Nonfunctioning Public Sector

By Chicago standards, Baghdad, along with almost all the rest of Iraq, is a catastrophe. For that matter, conditions are disastrous even by the looser standards of places like Beirut [Lebanon], Bogotá [capital of Colombia], and Bombay [India]. Reports from the scene are in general agreement on the

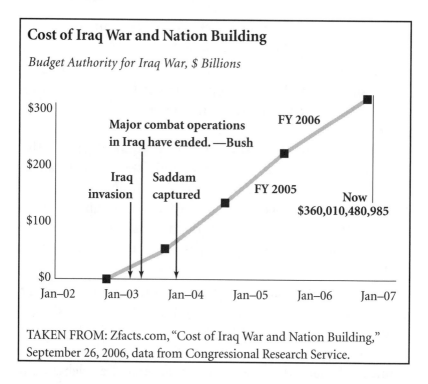

Cost of Iraq War and Nation Building

Budget Authority for Iraq War, $ Billions

TAKEN FROM: Zfacts.com, "Cost of Iraq War and Nation Building," September 26, 2006, data from Congressional Research Service.

essentials. Iraq is well rid of the murderous regime of Saddam Hussein. But the blithe assumptions of the Iraq war's Pentagon architects—that a grateful Iraqi nation, with a little help from American know-how and Iraqi oil cash, would quickly pick itself up, dust itself off, and start all over again—are as shattered as the buildings that used to house Saddam's favorite restaurants. In Baghdad, and in many other Iraqi cities and towns, civic society has degenerated into a Hobbesian [after 17th-century English author Thomas Hobbes, meaning selfish, uncivilized competition] state of nature. Despite the heroic efforts of a scattered minority of midlevel Iraqi civil servants, the services that make urban life viable are functioning, at best, erratically. More often, they do not function at all. "In the most palpable of ways, the American promise of a new Iraq is floundering on the inability of the American occupiers to provide basic services," the [*New York*] *Times*'s Neela Banerjee reported a few days ago. (Perhaps with an eye to educating her White House readers, she added that Baghdad is "about the size of metropolitan Houston.") Telephones are dead. Electricity and running water work, if at all, for only a few hours a day. Because the water pumps are hobbled by power outages, raw sewage is pouring into the Tigris River and is leaking into the fresh-water system, spreading disease and making the city stink. Hospitals that are secure enough to remain open overflow with patients, but they are short of food, medical supplies, and personnel. (Only a fifth of prewar health staffs are showing up for work.) Worst of all is the pervasive, well-founded fear of crime. Armed thugs rule the streets, especially in the pitch-black nights. "Amid such privations," Banerjee writes, "one of the few things that thrives now in Baghdad, at least, is a deepening distrust and anger toward the United States."

Immoral Morality

It's tempting to suggest that the Bush Administration is failing to provide Iraq with functioning, efficient, reliable public services because it doesn't *believe* in functioning, efficient, reliable public services—doesn't believe that they should exist, and doesn't really believe that they can exist. The [Republican] ideologues in Washington—not only in the White House but also in the Republican congressional leadership, in the faction that dominates the Supreme Court, and in the conservative press and think tanks—believe in free markets, individual initiative, and private schools and private charity as substitutes for public provision. They believe that the armed individual citizen is the ultimate guarantor of public safety. They do not, at bottom, believe that society, through the mechanisms of democratic government, has a moral obligation to provide care for the sick, food for the hungry, shelter for the homeless, and education for all; and to the extent that they tolerate such activities they do so grudgingly, out of political necessity. They believe that the private sector is sovereign, and that taxes are a species of theft. To paraphrase [Pierre Joseph] Proudhon [19th-century philosopher and anarchist], *les impôts, c'est le vol* [taxation is theft].

In a way, Iraq has become a theme park of conservative policy nostrums. There are no burdensome government regulations. Health and safety inspectors and environmental busybodies are nowhere to be seen. The Ministry of Finance, Iraq's equivalent of the Internal Revenue Service, is a scorched ruin. Museums and other cultural institutions, having been largely emptied of their contents, no longer have much use for public subsidies. Gun control is being kept within reasonable limits. (Although the occupying authorities are trying to discourage possession of heavy munitions, AK-47s and other assault weapons—guns of the type whose manufacture [former House majority leader] Tom DeLay and most of the House Republicans plan to re-legalize back home—have been given a pass.) And, in the absence of welfare programs and other free-lunch giveaways, faith-based initiatives are flourishing. The faith in question may be Iranian-style militant Shiism, but at least it's fundamentalist.

A Hostility to Nation-Building

The Bush Administration no longer flaunts its contempt for nation-building abroad, but it remains resolutely hostile to nation-building at home. Its domestic policy consists almost solely of a never-ending campaign to reduce the taxes of the very rich. Not all of this largesse will be paid for by loading debt onto future generations. Some of it is being paid for right now, by cuts in public services—cuts that outweigh the spare-change breaks for less affluent families which the Administration, in selling its successive tax elixirs, has had to include in order to suppress the electorate's gag reflex. The pain is especially acute at the state level, where net federal help is in decline. States are cancelling school construction, truncating the academic year, increasing class sizes, and eliminating preschool and after-school programs. Health benefits are being slashed, and a million people will likely lose coverage altogether. In many states, even cops are getting laid off.

As it happens, these are the very kinds of public services that America's proconsuls are promising to bring to Iraq. Of course, being nice to Iraq does not necessarily require the United States to be nice to itself. Nor does denying medicine to kids in Texas require denying it to kids in Baghdad. The connection is more karmic than causal. But it's also political. Whatever one may think of the global democratic-imperial ambitions of the present Administration, they cannot long coexist with the combination of narrow greed and public neglect it thinks sufficient for what it is pleased to call the homeland. At some point—the sooner the better—a critical mass of Americans will notice.

"Iraqi personnel can implement any reconstruction project with little or no onsite help from foreign contractors."

Iraqi Nation-Building Can Reconstruct Iraq

Jason Yossef Ben-Meir

In this viewpoint, Jason Yossef Ben-Meir argues that rebuilding Iraq requires a new strategy to succeed. The failures of the current Iraq nation-building program are due to a bureaucratic, top-down model that leaves most Iraqis on the sidelines. Ben-Meir's bottom-up approach relies on local know-how and materials, and Iraqi communities who prioritize their own reconstruction needs. This change in U.S. policy would lead to successful nation-building one community at a time. Jason Yossef Ben-Meir teaches sociology at the University of New Mexico.

As you read, consider the following questions:

1. According to Ben-Meir, what are the failures of the U.S.-led reconstruction effort in Iraq through 2006?

2. What made the Moroccan example of nation-building successful, according to Ben-Meir?

3. How much money would the United States need to spend on reconstruction if Ben-Muir's "bottom-up" strategy of nation-building was adopted?

The new strategy of the United States in Iraq does not include an extensive overhaul of reconstruction efforts at this critical time. Very little money is now being appropriated for reconstruction. As the Iraq Study Group [a 10-person, bipartisan commission appointed by Congress in March 2006 to assess the situation in Iraq] Report explains, of the $21 billion to date that has been appropriated for the "Iraq Relief and Reconstruction Fund" (IRRF), $16 billion has been spent and the remaining funds have been committed. The administration requested $750 million for 2007, and the President Bush's new proposal is to add $1.2 billion to that.

This failure to address Iraq's economic needs in a new way is extremely unfortunate for the Iraqis and for U.S. standing there and throughout the region.

However, with a Democratic Congress now in control [after winning a Congressional majority in the 2006 elections], and the Bush administration saying it's willing to reassess the situation with "fresh eyes," the United States still has the potential to finally apply in Iraq a basic lesson about how to implement successful development and reconstruction projects. Local community members in rural villages and neighborhoods need to identify and self-manage development projects that meet their priority needs. This bottom-up approach should borrow from the lessons of experience of Morocco.

A Tale of Two Approaches

The current reconstruction experience in Iraq is overwhelmingly negative. Billions of dollars have been wasted. Projects have gone uncompleted or sabotaged. Corruption is commonplace. Funds from the IRRF have been largely disbursed to private U.S. firms. And their top-down management style, combined with security concerns, has led them to make reconstruction decisions with little or no consultation with Iraqi community members. The enormous involvement of U.S. firms is counter-productive and difficult to justify. The UN report evaluating Iraq's reconstruction from 1991–2002 concludes: "Iraqi personnel can implement any reconstruction project with little or no onsite help from foreign contractors."

Part of the new U.S. strategy in Iraq is to expand American reconstruction teams. First there is the challenge of recruiting volunteers. Then there is the expense of providing them with administrative infrastructure and the much higher cost of helping to ensure their security. In the past, security cost as much as 30% of project funding. A new "key tactical shift" to deal with the security of the reconstruction teams is to integrate them with military combat teams. However, the mission of the reconstruction teams is more of the same. Their expansion is not essential for the promotion of the locally empowering bottom-up approach to reconstruction.

Although an exception, the bottom-up community-based approach has guided the reconstruction work of some development agencies in Iraq. CHF International, a Maryland-based nonprofit organization, has been particularly successful. Its Middle East director, Bruce Parmelee, observed after completing hundreds of projects on small budgets: "People won't attack projects that they feel ownership of." Community projects require smaller budgets because of lower management costs and contributions from local people, such as labor. With the entire community involved, creating great accountability and oversight, corruption is diminished.

There is an erroneous tendency among policy-makers, which appears also in the Iraq Study Group Report, to separate reconstruction efforts from the process of achieving a political settlement. In fact, bottom-up reconstruction is a federalist democratic process. It strengthens the ability of localities

Focus on Iraqis

The reconstruction of Iraq must focus on the expertise and enthusiasm of Iraqi people, according to postwar reconstruction experts at the University of York.

Sultan Barakat and Gareth Wardell run the Postwar Reconstruction and Development Unit (PRDU) at the University. . . .

"Lessons learnt from all over the world in the last 20 years show that running reconstruction activities as though they're a military campaign—from the top down—are expensive, unsustainable and ineffective," says Dr Barakat.

BBC, "Grassroots Approach to Rebuild Iraq."
www.bbc.co.uk.

to make their own development decisions in an inclusive, dialogue-based way. If the central government provides financial and logistical support for this empowering approach to reconstruction, localities will not want to completely sever their ties to the national government. This can provide the basis for the local and regional relationships with the central authority that the Iraqi people are struggling to create. Joseph Gregoire, leader of a Provisional Reconstruction Team in Iraq, recently suggested, in *The Washington Post* that "projects tend to overcome sectarian differences."

Reconstruction and Reconciliation

Bottom-up reconstruction and reconciliation also overlap operationally. Both require direct dialogue among community members, recognition among participants of each other's experiences, needs, and interests, and both are processes that use third-party facilitation to ensure a constructive experience. Further, in successful reconciliation models, once the parties to a conflict acknowledge each other's pain and suffering and express regret, the process moves to joint development efforts that help meet local people's basic needs.

Reconstruction and reconciliation, therefore, are opposite sides of the same coin. For either to be achieved both must be advanced, as what happened, for example, in Morocco. In 1999, Morocco was the first country in the Arab world to create a Truth and Reconciliation Commission, which brought to light serious past injustices for national discussion. Consistent with a genuine reconciliation process, Morocco also launched the National Initiative for Human Development to promote local development and self-reliance. The Iraq Study Group Report suggests that "Egypt should be encouraged to foster the national reconciliation process in Iraq." I propose that Morocco, with more experience, should play a key role.

Embarking on a reconciliation process while Iraq is experiencing daily, murderous sectarian violence presents challenges well beyond what Morocco faced when it moved forward on its own national reconciliation. To be sure, many Iraqis may feel fearful about participating in reconciliation dialogue out of personal safety concerns. The important advantage, however, to connecting reconciliation processes to locally driven reconstruction is that these processes are decentralized and not highly visible targets for those who oppose them. Therefore, while community-based reconciliation and reconstruction are very effective and empowering processes for their participants, they are also dispersed and don't present the conspicuous targets that insurgents often choose to maximize the level of fear among the Iraqi public. Furthermore, U.S. military commanders understand that "counterinsurgency" involves cultivating popular support. Reconstruction projects supported by the United States that are based on the self-defined interests of local Iraqi people are powerful acts of public diplomacy and further marginalize extremists.

Funding Grassroots Rebuilding

In a situation where time is so crucial, one may question if bottom-up reconstruction would make a significant difference in the short term. But unlike top-down approaches dependent on foreign contractors, the bottom-up approach relies on local know-how and materials, thus permitting immediate implementation if funding is available. To begin, local third-party facilitators need to be trained. They catalyze and assist community meetings where local people determine which new projects to establish. Effective training can be done in groups of 20 (including teachers, government and non-government personnel, local politicians, and citizens) over a two-week period, using a progressive "experiential" pedagogy.

A range of technical specialties among members of Provisional Reconstruction Teams, which makes recruitment even more cumbersome, is not what is needed. The necessary technical skills required to operate specific projects are available locally. Rather, Iraq needs trainers in participatory tools that can help communities design, implement, and manage their own projects. These trainers would be knowledgeable in negotiating consensus and participation within communities. President Bush's new strategy does indeed include increased "quick response" funding for local reconstruction projects. Such funds can help implement projects that local members of communities determine for themselves. But the bottom-up approach needs a greater financial boost.

A "Bottom-Up" Approach

A commitment by the United States of $5 billion for reconstruction, an amount called for by the Iraq Study Group, if applied in the bottom-up way could enable more than 10 million Iraqis to reap profound socio-economic benefits, with significant results in just a few months. A Senior Advisor for Economic Reconstruction in Iraq who reports to the president and with a broad mandate to coordinate reconstruction among

U.S. agencies and Iraqi counterparts—a recommendation from the Iraq Study Group as well—can significantly expedite bottom-up reconstruction.

We have seen the ineffectual and corrupt outcomes of top-down reconstruction. Now we need to turn to what we know works, the bottom-up community approach.

> *"Our mission in Iraq should not be nation building. It should be destruction of our enemies to the point where they agree to fight no more."*

Destroy the Enemy in Iraq, Do Not Nation-Build

Ed Marek

Ed Marek argues in this viewpoint for an aggressive destruction of the enemy in Iraq that precludes nation-building. He believes that the U.S. Congress should issue a formal declaration of war against our enemies in Iraq. Democracy, he argues, cannot be achieved in Iraq through the nation-building efforts of the State Department and their contracted nongovernmental organizations (NGOs). Ed Marek is the editor and founder of Talking Proud, *an online magazine that he developed. He served 20 years in the United States Air Force.*

As you read, consider the following questions:

1. Does the author believe that one of the goals resulting from the invasion of Iraq should be creation of an Iraqi democracy?

2. The author argues that democracy building has started under false pretenses. Why?

Ed Marek, "No Nation Building—Destroy Our Enemies in Iraq," *Talking Proud*, December 14, 2005. www.talkingproud.us. Reproduced by permission.

3. Should the United States be termed "an occupation force" in Iraq, according to Marek?

The president [George W. Bush] said [on December 14, 2005], "We are in Iraq because our goal has always been ... to leave a free and democratic Iraq. . ." This editor objects. Running for office in 2000, Mr. Bush promised no nation-building. Iraq was a threat to the US. That's why we invaded. Iraq has not yet surrendered to us. That's why we're still at war and fighting. Our mission in Iraq should not be nation building. It should be destruction of our enemies to the point where they agree to fight no more. Please, Mr. President. Destroy them.

President Bush sure makes it hard for guys like me to support him. I am doing my very best to stick by his side but he's very close to pushing me over the cliff.

Speaking on December 14, 2005 before the Woodrow Wilson International Center for Scholars in Washington, Mr. Bush said the following:

> "We are in Iraq today because our goal has always been more than the removal of a brutal dictator. It is to leave a free and democratic Iraq in his place."

The Goal in Iraq Should Not Be Democracy

I have to tell you, Mr. President, I have worked hard to pay close attention to all this, and I never understood our invasion of Iraq to be for the purpose of leaving a free and democratic Iraq.

While it would be nice for Iraq to be free and democratic, I surely did not understand leaving it in that kind of shape has always been "our goal," always a requirement. I am sorry. If that was a requirement from the beginning, "our goal," I plain missed it.

Facing the Truth

"We are losing in Iraq and Afghanistan," asserts former senior CIA analyst Michael Scheuer, "because the political leaders of both parties—and their politically correct acolytes in the media, the academy and the general officer corps—refuse to square with the American people about the enemy's motivation."

That motivation is their 1,400-year-old faith, said Scheuer, who closely tracked Muslim terrorists like Osama bin Laden over the last decade.

Indeed, the biggest myth going is that Islam has been "hijacked" by the terrorists. No, the only thing that's been hijacked is the truth about fundamentalist, radical Islam, which makes holy war against infidels a sacred duty for Muslims.

Investor's Business Daily Editors, Opinion/Editorial,
"Drop the Gloves," February 2, 2007. www.investors.com.

No Nation-Building

It would be easy to understand why I might miss it. I would never have expected that as a goal from Mr. Bush. One of the reasons I voted for him in 2000 was that he promised no nation building. During a debate with Mr. Gore on October 11, 2000 in Winston-Salem, North Carolina, Mr. Bush said this:

> "I don't think our troops ought to be used for what's called nation-building. . . . I think what we need to do is convince people who live in the lands they live in to build the nations. Maybe I'm missing something here. I mean, we're going to have a kind of nation-building corps from America? Absolutely not."

I agreed then with that and I agree now with that. No nation-building. Right on, Mr. President!

At the time of our invasion buildup, I saw [Iraqi dictator] Saddam Hussein and his government as serious threats to US national security. Initially, we thought Iraq had weapons of mass destruction that might be used against us. I have accepted that we have not found such weapons, yet. But that did not mark the end of my world. I believed and still believe that Hussein intended to get them and would use them against us in some fashion. So taking him and his henchmen down was fine by me. I roar with laughter watching the old goat whine on international television about how [he] is not getting a fair hearing. If I were in charge, I'd tell the guards to leave the jail doors open and shoot him while he is running out the back door. [Saddam Hussein was hanged on December 30, 2006, after being found guilty of crimes against humanity by an Iraqi court.]

Iraq Never Surrendered

But when we took him down, what happened? Did his government surrender unconditionally? No. When we caught Hussein, did he sign an unconditional surrender agreement? No. Did we demand these things of him at the time we jailed him? I do not know for sure, but I suspect not. To my mind, then, we remain in a state of war against Iraq. We must keep pressing for destruction of our enemies in Iraq to the point where they will fight us no more. Absent that, we remain at war.

I commend an article by Gregg Easterbrook to your attention. It was published by *The New Republic* on July 5, 2004, and was titled, "Sweet surrender." Easterbrook said this:

> There may be a simple, overlooked, and incredibly basic reason why the fighting in Iraq refuses to end: Namely, there was never a surrender. Saddam Hussein's government never formally capitulated.

Easterbrook is correct. Iraq as a nation has not admitted defeat, it has not agreed to stop fighting, and therefore many of its citizens have not ceased warfare against us. In addition, just as we have foreign allies, these enemies have foreign allies and they too are fighting against us. That's why the war goes on.

The United States Should Declare War

I do not accept the argument that Iraq turning to democracy will stop the fighting. Destroying our enemies in Iraq to the point where they can or will fight no more is the only way to stop the fighting. Just as I want our government to formally declare war against these people, so too I want our military forces to defeat and destroy these enemies until they get down on their knees and beg for an unconditional surrender.

As I think about all this, I am not sure it to be correct to call us an occupation force. Ours is a fighting force that still has the job of forcing a formal capitulation of our enemies in Iraq. They must be forced to surrender unconditionally and sign our terms of agreement.

Forget this nation-building stuff from the [U.S.] State Department and all the do-good nonsense that comes from those State Department supported non-government organizations (NGOs) occupying all that luxurious office space on Connecticut Avenue [in Washington, DC]. Please do this, Mr. President. You promised us no nation building—keep that promise.

Focus on Destruction of the Enemy

With regard to the war in Iraq, I continue to stand by my president's and our troops' sides to join our military forces with those of our allies, including the new Iraqi "freedom fighting" army and police, with the objective of destroying our enemies in Iraq, and demanding they get down on their sorry ass knees and surrender unconditionally. If all our Islamic enemies want to come to Iraq to fight, then I say, come on in and fight; we can get the whole job done in just one location. But we must insist on unconditional surrender, wherever we engage these bastards.

If democracy comes to Iraq, that's nice, and I will be among the first to commend the Iraqi people, but what I want is what all Americans should want, the destruction of our enemies.

That's the mission, not nation-building. Please, Mr. President.

> "The ongoing war in Iraq has proven that any plan for political democracy is insufficient without a viable plan for building economic democracy."

Nation-Building Will Empower Iraqi Citizens

Center for Economic and Social Justice

The Center for Economic and Social Justice argues in this viewpoint that successful nation-building in Iraq necessitates forming political democracy through economic justice. The center's model is called "The Just Third Way," a rejection of traditional capitalist and socialist economies in favor of decentralized and equal economic opportunity—for instance, the sharing of oil revenues amongst all Iraqis—allowing its citizens to rebuild the multiethnic, multireligious society the Iraq nation has always been. The Center for Economic and Social Justice is a think tank specializing in understanding the root causes of worldwide economic and social injustice, and promoting new thinking to transform injustice into successful societies.

As you read, consider the following questions:

1. The authors argue that there is a "fatal omission" in typical nation-building projects. What is it?

Center for Economic and Social Justice, "A New Model of Nation-Building for Citizens of Iraq," *www.cesj.org*, July 27, 2005. Reproduced by permission.

2. What do the authors claim as the advantage to diversifying capital (money through credit, loans, and oil revenues) throughout Iraqi society instead of through traditional democratic governance?

3. The authors argue that every Iraqi citizen should receive free oil shares from the country's existing oil production facilities to spur individual wealth and nation-building. They also contend that Iraq as a whole would benefit from UN support for a free trade exemption. What is the exemption based on?

[A]fter the U.S. and coalition forces invaded Iraq [in 2003] and captured Saddam Hussein [in December 2003], the cost of the war . . . , in blood and dollars, continues to mount.

The June 30, 2004 transfer of "sovereignty" to the Iraqi people has not yet brought about a government that can secure the "life, liberty and property" of its citizens. There is still no clear exit strategy for U.S. troops that would avoid leaving Iraq in chaos and civil war. No official plan for economic reconstruction [has] been offered by the U.S., its allies, or the U.N. that could unify the various factions in Iraq and provide for a broad sharing of ownership and economic power among all Iraqi citizens.

The [President George W.] Bush Administration continues to push for political democracy in Iraq. There is, however, mounting skepticism among critics that political democracy can work in the Islamic world. The ongoing war in Iraq has proven that any plan for political democracy is insufficient without a viable plan for building economic democracy. Such a plan requires an Iraqi model of what President Bush called an "ownership society."

Rebuilding Consistent with Islam

Tailoring it to the specific circumstances of Iraq, the Iraqi political and religious leadership should unleash a bold "Peace through Justice" offensive to reinforce the government's counter-terrorism initiatives. [We argue] a specific "first step" proposal with a powerful message that, if properly communicated by respected Iraqi leaders, cannot fail to capture the attention and raise the hopes of every Iraqi. Centered on who should own and receive profits from the nation's oil resources, this proposal deserves serious consideration by thoughtful leaders and citizens ready to explore a truly different paradigm that is consistent with Islam, one based on ownership and economic justice for every citizen.

With the vacuum of ideas being filled by growing hatred and bloodshed, the time has come to consider [a new] concept . . . and ask, "Why not?"

People in developing countries are increasingly rejecting capitalist and socialist models of development as power-concentrating and exploitative, or outmoded and inefficient. The Just Third Way, in contrast, is a nation-building model based on the equal opportunity of every citizen to acquire and possess productive capital assets within an economy that decentralizes economic power. The new model provides a stable foundation for an effective and religiously pluralistic democracy. It offers a viable and politically unifying framework for all Iraqi citizens to work and prosper together, regardless of their religious, ethnic, cultural and other differences.

Empowering the Citizen Economy

The new model addresses a "fatal omission" in conventional approaches to nation-building whose exclusionary policies engender a growing gap between the rich and poor, concentration of power and ownership within a small elite, corruption and abuses of power at all levels, and instability within society.

The leading edge of the new strategic framework is economic, attacking directly the root causes of terrorism and the basis of its support among the populace. It answers the demands of all Iraqi citizens for justice and an end to systemic poverty and oppression. It creates systematically a true nation of owners.

This strategy promotes the growing economic sovereignty and empowerment of each citizen—as a worker, as a consumer and as a capital owner. Economic governance and accountability are structurally diffused from the bottom-up by protecting existing private property rights and by spreading throughout society equal opportunity to acquire new and transferred productive capital assets. Universal access to capital ownership would enhance the economic well-being and self-determination of the people, and reduce the tendency toward corruption and abuses of power associated with any form of monopoly power.

Building Economic Self-Sufficiency

It sets up the legal and constitutional infrastructure for moving quickly to a high-growth, free market system. It is based on the four pillars of a just market economy: (1) expanded capital ownership, (2) limited economic power of the state, (3) restoration of free trade and open markets for determining just prices, just wages and just profits, and (4) restoration of private property in all means of production.

Because of its emphasis on infrastructural re-engineering (particularly with respect to central banking, capital credit, and land and natural resources development), this framework would radically reduce the cost of reconstruction of Iraq, allowing for low-cost internal means of financing the reconstruction. This would reduce the cost to the U.S. taxpayer, the U.N. and those countries supporting the effort in Iraq.

It would help Iraq become economically self-sufficient as soon as possible, providing the basis for a stable, independent, and democratic government that would serve as a model for other nations in the Middle East and around the world.

Local Initiatives and Human Rights

Iraq's reconstruction process ought to take place in a way that respects the long-denied basic human rights of all Iraqis. There is already ample reason to doubt how much importance the occupation regime will place on the protection of those rights. In addition, a progressive humanitarian agenda must recognize the critical importance of encouraging local initiative in the rebuilding of the country, thereby strengthening an emerging Iraqi civil society. Iraqi civil organizations will doubtless promote varied visions of a new Iraq. Even amidst this challenging and contradictory diversity, a true humanitarian agenda will honor local initiative.

Grassroots International Editors,
"The Iraq Challenge of Humanitarian Response,"
May 2003. www.grassrootsonline.org.

Transfer Free Oil Shares to All Iraqis

Denationalize the oil fields of Iraq, as a catalyst for building a new "Just Third Way" economy. Transfer the ownership and control of all oil reserves and natural resources within the borders of Iraq from the Iraqi National Oil Company to a newly formed, professionally managed, limited liability joint stock corporation. All Iraqis would automatically receive free, as a right of citizenship from birth to death, an equal number of *non-transferable* shares in the new corporation. All citizens would be guaranteed first-class shareholder rights to the profits and voting control over the board of directors and management of the new company. All profits except for operating reserves would be paid out fully and periodically as dividends to each shareholder.

To meet all costs and services of government at the national, provincial and local levels, taxes on such dividend incomes would be withheld by the corporation before distributing the balance of dividends to each citizen. The shares of those who die would be retired to the General Fund or redistributed to new-borns, returning Iraqi exiles and newly naturalized citizens, who would receive an equal number of shares as existing shareholders.

The new corporation would encourage market forces in setting prices throughout the economy by offering, through a competitive bidding process, concessions and leases for exploration, drilling, infrastructural engineering and construction, processing and marketing oil and other natural resource activities. Preferential treatment would be given to competitive operating companies that are broadly owned by Iraqi citizens.

A Foundation for Wealth-Building

To lay the foundations for Iraq's future economy, new industrial, agricultural and commercial demonstration projects (for example, using advanced alternative energy technologies that produce power and water from sea water and waste), could be launched and financed in ways that encourage wider share ownership among Iraqi workers and other stakeholders.

Future government revenues would then flow from the bottom-up from increasing citizen incomes. This would make government more dependent economically on its citizens, rather than perpetuating the previous top-down dependency of the people on a political elite. A single rate of taxation on all incomes above poverty levels would balance government budgets, achieve greater accountability, transparency and democratic participation in governance at all levels, and radically reduce future risks of public sector corruption or future coups.

Personal share accounts (like Individual Retirement Accounts in the U.S.) would be set up within local banks for each worker and every citizen of Iraq to accumulate income-producing capital assets, sheltered from any taxes until assets or income are distributed for personal consumption. The equity accumulation accounts would also be given the power to borrow interest-free, non-recourse productive credit on behalf of the citizen.

This "capital credit" would be used exclusively by citizens to purchase new shares issued by new or growing Iraqi enterprises to finance the expansion and modernization needs of a growing Iraqi economy. The debt for purchasing the newly issued growth shares would be secured and repaid by the projected dividends on those shares (as with leveraged employee stock ownership plans[1] in the U.S.).

One cautionary note: Experience with employee stock ownership plans has shown that it is not sufficient merely to give people ownership and expect any significant change in their behavior and value systems. It is essential that, during the planning and implementation phases of a national ownership strategy, management systems be introduced that encourage a servant leadership philosophy and structures and processes for diffusing economic power, ownership and participation. One such system called "Justice-Based Management" systematically builds internal ownership cultures necessary to educate all stakeholders and maintain the continued deconcentration of power and accountability of managers to the worker—and citizen—shareholders.

Building Economic Growth in Iraq

The constitution drafted by Iraqis [and approved by referendum wrote on October 15, 2005] should reflect all the rights contained in the UN *Declaration of Human Rights*, particularly Article 17 (acknowledging every person's right to own property individually or in association with others). The new Iraqi constitution should include the provision that as a fundamental right of citizenship every citizen is guaranteed access

---

1. Leveraged employee stock ownership is a type of pension and profit-sharing plan that borrows money to purchase stock in the company or issue the ability to purchase common stock. It ensures that majority ownership remains in friendly hands.

to the social means (i.e., money and interest-free productive credit) for acquiring and possessing income-producing property. All tax, credit, property, corporation, insurance, inheritance and related laws should, if necessary, be reconstituted to conform to the constitution and to establish institutions supporting economic democracy and the universal right to private property and protection of the rights of property.

The discount power of the central bank in Iraq should be restructured to encourage non-inflationary private-sector productive growth through the creation of interest-free money for local banks for promoting more universal citizen access to capital credit for financing new investments.

U.S. and other countries should introduce a resolution into the U.N. General Assembly to treat Iraq as a "global free trade zone" whose imports and exports would be exempt from all trade barriers and tariffs of other countries. In this way the international community could provide a major catalyst for "Peace Through Justice" in Iraq and throughout the Middle East.

| "Another concept whose bitter falsity has been painfully revealed in Iraq is 'nation-building.'"

Nation-Building Will Oppress Iraqi Citizens

Thomas Sowell

Thomas Sowell is senior fellow on public policy at the Hoover Institution at Stanford University and author of Black Rednecks and White Liberals. *Sowell argues that Iraq is an artificially created new nation, like other states in the Balkans and Africa, lacking the cultural cement of history and justice. The failure of nation-building in Iraq, he argues, stems from the peculiar American idea that glorifies diversity at the expense of a cohesive, unified state, which has doomed U.S. nation-building efforts, promoting an ongoing war and continuing the oppression of ordinary Iraqis.*

As you read, consider the following questions:

1. What has made Iraq so difficult to pacify and reconstruct, even after a decisive U.S. military victory, according to Sowell?

Thomas Sowell, "Diversity's Oppressions," *Opinion Journal*, October 30, 2006. www .opinionjournal.com. Copyright © Dow Jones & Company, Inc. All rights reserved. Reproduced by permission.

2. Does the author believe that dictatorships can hold newly created nations together?

3. Does the author believe that the United States is in the nation-building phase of Iraqi unification or at war? In his view, what are the consequences of that understanding?

Iraq is not the first war with ugly surprises and bloody setbacks. Even World War II, idealized in retrospect as it never was at the time—the war of "the greatest generation"—had a long series of disasters for Americans before victory was finally achieved.

The war began for Americans with the disaster at Pearl Harbor, followed by the tragic horror of the Bataan death march [Japanese enforced march of surrendered U.S. and Filipino prisoners of war during WWII that led to the death of 16,000 POWs], the debacle at the Kasserine Pass [battles fought in a two-mile gap in the Atlas mountains of Tunisia during WWII, which the Germans won over Allied forces] and, even on the eve of victory, being caught completely by surprise by a devastating German counterattack that almost succeeded at the Battle of the Bulge [surprise German attack against Allied forces at the end of WWII, resulting in the highest casualty rate for the United States. during the war].

The Hard Lesson of Pacification

Other wars—our own and other nations'—have likewise been full of nasty surprises and mistakes that led to bloodbaths. Nevertheless, the Iraq war has some special lessons for our time, lessons that both the left and the right need to acknowledge, whether or not they will.

What is it that has made Iraq so hard to pacify, even after a swift and decisive military victory? In one word: diversity.

That word has become a sacred mantra, endlessly repeated for years on end, without a speck of evidence being asked for or given to verify the wonderful benefits it is assumed to produce.

The Disasters of Diversity and Nation-Building

Worse yet, Iraq is only the latest in a long series of catastrophes growing out of diversity. These include "ethnic cleansing" in the Balkans [a series of violent conflicts between, mostly, Serbians against Croatians, Macedonians, and Albanians from about 1999 to 2004], genocide in Rwanda [the killing of about 500,000 ethnic Tutsis by two extremist Hutu tribe militias in this African country from April to July 1994], and the Sudan [the conflict in Darfur, a western region of Sudan, Africa, where the Janjaweed militia are accused of massacring endemic, agricultural tribes], the million lives destroyed in intercommunal violence when India became independent [from British colonial rule] in 1947 and the even larger number of Armenians slaughtered by Turks during World War I [during a forced evacuation of Armenians from the Ottoman Empire between 1915 and 1917].

Despite much gushing about how we should "celebrate diversity," America's great achievement has not been in having diversity but in taming its dangers that have run amok in many other countries. Americans have by no means escaped diversity's oppressions and violence, but we have reined them in.

Another concept whose bitter falsity has been painfully revealed in Iraq is "nation-building." People are not building blocks, however much some may flatter themselves that they can arrange their fellow human beings' lives the way you can arrange pieces on a chess board.

Artificial Nations

The biggest and most fatuous example of nation-building occurred right after World War I, when the allied victors dismembered the Habsburg Empire and the Ottoman Empire. Woodrow Wilson assigned a young Walter Lippman [U.S. journalist, founding editor of *The New Republic* magazine and adviser to President Wilson] to sit down with maps and population statistics and start drawing lines that would define new nations.

Iraq is one of those new nations. Like other artificial creations in the Balkans, Africa and elsewhere, it has never had the cohesion of nations that evolved over the centuries out of the experiences of peoples who worked out their own modi vivendi [way of life] in one way or another.

[Josip Broz] Tito's dictatorship held Yugoslavia together, as other dictatorships held together other peoples forced into becoming a nation by the decisions of outsiders who drew their boundaries on maps and in some cases—Nigeria, for example—even gave them their national name.

Even before 9/11, there were some neoconservatives who talked about our achieving "national greatness" by creating democratic nations in various parts of the world.

Free Societies Require Long Evolution

How much influence their ideas have had on the actual course of events is probably something that will not be known in our generation. But we can at least hope that the Iraq tragedy will chasten the hubris behind notions of "nation-building" and chasten also the pious dogmatism of those who hype "diversity" at every turn, in utter disregard of its actual consequences at home or abroad. Free societies have prerequisites, and history has not given all peoples those prerequisites, which took centuries to evolve in the West.

However we got into Iraq, we cannot undo history—even recent history—by simply pulling out and leaving events to take their course in that strife-torn country. Whether or not we "stay the course," terrorists are certainly going to stay the course in Iraq and around the world.

Deny Terrorists an Iraq Victory

Political spin may say that Iraq has nothing to do with the war on terror, but the terrorists themselves quite obviously believe otherwise, as they converge on that country with lethal and suicidal resolve.

Whether we want to or not, we cannot unilaterally end the war with international terrorists. Giving the terrorists an epoch-making victory in Iraq would only shift the location where we must face them or succumb to them.

Abandoning Iraqi allies to their fate would ensure that other nations would think twice before becoming or remaining our allies. With a nuclear Iran looming on the horizon [Iran claims to be developing nuclear power for electricity, but many in the world community believe they are seeking a nuclear bomb], we are going to need all the allies we can get.

> *"In this occupation, the US and its allies'*
> *primary goal is not to rebuild what*
> *they have destroyed; it's to make a fast*
> *buck."*

Faking Nation-Building in Iraq

Herbert Docena

Herbert Docena is a staff writer for the Asia Times. *Docena argues that "It's the stupidity, stupid," that is causing the failure of Iraqi nation-building. Contracts, for instance, were written that only allowed American spare parts to be used on infrastructure projects, originally built in Russia, France, Germany, and Japan. The money, Docena argues, has flowed from the U.S. government to top-heavy, cash-rich American companies, who are providing needed technical expertise, but none is reaching the average Iraqi reconstruction ministries.*

As you read, consider the following questions:

1. According to the author, have the Iraqis ever shown that they can rapidly reconstruct their own country's infrastructure?

Herbert Docena, "Iraq Reconstruction's Bottom-Line," *Asia Times* online, December 25, 2003. www.atimes.com. Reproduced by permission.

2. Do large American companies like Halliburton have the engineering expertise needed to rebuild Iraq, according to Docena?

3. According to Iraqis, has the United States provided enough money to rebuild the electrical grid in Iraq, according to the viewpoint?

4. The U.S. Army Corps of Engineers spokesperson in the viewpoint describes the incentive for U.S. companies to rebuild nations in dangerous locations. What is it?

Even if the occupation were working perfectly well, it would still be wrong. This has become trite commentary among Iraqis who bitterly want the occupation of their country to fail but, at the same time, also earnestly hope that the reconstruction of their country succeeds. Still, no matter how hard the occupiers try to make the reconstruction go right, the US and its corporations still have no right staying here.

At night, most of downtown Baghdad is still in darkness [as of 2003] with only the blue and red police sirens lighting the streets and the only sound that of intermittent gunfire puncturing the silence—definitely not a picture of a festive, newly liberated capital. With most of Iraq suffering from power interruptions lasting an average of 16 hours daily, it's a little hard to party in the dark. How many US soldiers does it take to change a light bulb? About 130,000 so far, but don't hold your breath.

Waiting for the Americans

South of the city, a double-columned queue of cars up to three kilometers in length snakes around street blocks and crosses a bridge over the Tigris before finally terminating at a barbed wired gasoline station protected by a Humvee and an armored tank. Come closing time, so as not to abandon the queue and line up all over again the following day, most of the car owners decide to leave their vehicles parked overnight, in a nightly vigil for gasoline in a country with the world's second-largest reserves of oil.

During the day, some of Iraq's 12 million unemployed hang out in front of Checkpoint 3 of the Green Zone, the heavily fortified headquarters of the Coalition Provisional Authority (CPA). The chances of an American accepting their resumes is next to nil, but they come every day anyway. Others try their luck loitering in the hotel lobbies, besieging journalists or non-government workers in need of drivers and translators.

With many unemployed former university professors, engineers and civil servants choosing to become cab drivers instead, Baghdad probably has the most educated taxi drivers per square kilometer in the world. Strike up a conversation and the cabbies will most likely tell you what seems to have become the conventional wisdom today: not even Saddam Hussein could have screwed up this badly.

Not that they want him back, but neither could they have expected the occupation forces to completely bungle such simple tasks as switching the lights back on. The lack of power is most Iraqis' number one gripe, but the list is long: uninstalled phone lines, shoddily repaired schools, clogged roads, uncollected garbage, defective sewerage, a nonexistent bureaucracy, mass unemployment and widespread poverty—the general chaos that Iraq is still in today.

How Hard Is It to Get the Lights On?

Iraqis are in broad agreement that life is deteriorating rather than improving. The prevailing sentiment is a complex mix of resentment and resignation, frustration and incredulity. On the one hand, Iraqis feel bitter about being occupied, and yet many are resigned to entrusting their day-to-day survival to the hands of the Americans. On the other hand, they could not quite believe how despite all the time and money, the world's sole superpower can't make the reconstruction process go right.

For it's part, the US says the Iraqis are expecting too much too soon. "The bottleneck is sheer time," explained Ted Morse, the CPA's coordinator for the Baghdad region. "Wherever you have had a true conflict situation, there is an impatience in that people think it can be done immediately. It cannot."

But Iraqis themselves have showed that it can. In 1991, after the first Gulf War and despite the United Nations-imposed sanctions, it took Iraq's bureaucrats and engineers only three months to restore electricity back to pre-war capacity, boasted Janan Behman, manager of Baghdad's Daura power station. Now after almost nine months and despite the involvement of US giant Bechtel, builders of the Hoover Dam and some of the world's biggest engineering works, Iraq's power sector is still only producing less than 20 percent or 3,600 MW out of the 20,000 MW required. A daily power interruption of two to three hours would be acceptable after nine months, but 16 hours?

A Scared and Inexperienced Occupation

The occupation forces would not admit this, of course, but much of the problem could be attributed to the successful efforts of the resistance to ensure that nothing works as long as an illegal occupation stays in place. The resistance has kept the authorities too busy dodging bombs to spare time for such trifling matters as providing Iraqis with jobs. With the resistance targeting not just combatants but also those profiting from the occupation, it's a little too much to expect contractors to go out of their tightly guarded bubbles and move around.

Bechtel employees, for example, only travel in military helicopters or armed convoys with at least one designated "shooter" in every vehicle. Now unless they find a way of transporting the power plants to the trailer camps where Bechtel employees live—averse as they are from going to the plants themselves—nothing much would really get done.

A lot of the mess could also be attributed to the sheer incompetence and lack of experience of the people running Iraq. Much has been said about how the administrators housed in the Green Zone have little or no experience whatsoever in public administration. There have also been various reports about the confusion and lack of coordination among the different agencies involved. Moreover, as in previous colonial administrations, it is often difficult to entice the best and the brightest to pack up, leave everything behind, relocate to some far-flung hardship post, only to be welcomed with guns.

But insecurity and incompetence, while part of the complete and complex picture, do not go far enough in explaining why the reconstruction effort has so far been an evident failure.

Refusing Occupation

First, while only 1 percent of those surveyed in a [2003] Gallup poll buy the line that the US came to establish democracy, the majority of the Iraqis are not actively fighting the occupation. While the resistance is growing, this is not an intifada [Palestinian uprising against Israeli occupation] yet. While a mere 6 percent of those surveyed believe the US is here to help, Iraqis who are in a position to assist in the reconstruction effort actually want to make it work, not so much to prop up the occupying forces, they say, but to ensure that oil and electricity are kept available. Iraqis may not necessarily like the Americans, but they would sure like some hot water in the morning [in] winter.

"If this is the system, then I have to follow," said Dathar al-Khshab, general director of the Daura oil refinery. It's the only way to keep things moving, then so be it, he said, echoing other utilities managers. Rank and file oil industry workers are likewise hesitant to shut down the refineries as a bargaining chip for negotiations and as a tactic to undermine the occupation. On the one hand, they know that this could paralyze the Americans. On the other, they are afraid of its effect on the Iraqi people. But asked whether they support the coalition forces, Hassan Jum'a, leader of the Southern Oil Company union, was firm: "You can't hide the moon. Every honest Iraqi should refuse the occupation."

Incompetence Is Not the Problem

The charge of incompetence is not completely convincing either because, for all the allegations of unfair competition and shadowy connections, it would be difficult to accuse Bechtel or Halliburton of not knowing what they are doing.

With projects scattered all over the globe, Bechtel is one of the world's biggest construction firms and it has achieved some of history's most awesome engineering feats. Halliburton, on the other hand, has been repairing oil wells and refineries around the world for decades. Even Iraqi officials readily acknowledge that, technically speaking, they should be in good hands with these American contractors. As the grudging respect gradually gives way to disappointment, Iraqis are even more baffled as to how these corporations could fail their expectations.

Another popular explanation making the rounds alleges that sabotaging the reconstruction is a conscious and deliberate effort on the part of the occupation forces to make the Iraqis completely dependent and subservient. Keeping a dog hungry not only keeps it from barking, it also makes the dog follow its master anywhere.

The problem with this theory is that due to the relatively decentralized reconstruction process involving dozens of contractors and sub-contractors, an explicit order for deliberate failure would have been almost impossible to secretly enforce. Moreover, faced with a mounting resistance, this tactic could

An Occupation of Puppets

[Iraqi activist Houzan Mahmoud is speaking] The US and the occupying powers, in my opinion, are protecting terrorist networks, rather than secular, progressive movements inside Iraq. The occupying forces were the first to prevent the Organization of Women's Freedom in Iraq from having a demonstration against the rapes and abductions. We were told that we are not allowed to have a demonstration without their permission. The first Union of the Unemployed in Iraq sit-in strikes in Baghdad, in the very beginning of the occupation—its leaders were arrested by the US occupying powers. So they don't want to see any progressive, militant, secular, egalitarian movement inside Iraq with a vision for a better future, for an alternative, for a government that is not a puppet of the US. They just want to put puppets there, they don't care what's happening to the society . . . what they care about is just their own interest. We are not protecting their interest, we are protecting the interest of the Iraqi people; that's why they don't want us to grow and they won't be any support to us at all.

Bill Weinberg, "'We Are Hope': Voices from the Secular Resistance Movement in Iraq," June 2006, interview of Houzan Mahmoud on WBAI radio, March 21, 2006, American Friends Service Committee. www.afsc.org.

be extremely risky because it undermines the effort to "win hearts and minds." Keeping a dog hungry could also turn it desperate and rabid.

The answer to the mystery of why the reconstruction has so far been botched could be less sinister.

Made in the USA

A clue lies at the Najibiya power station in Basra, Iraq's second largest city located south of Baghdad. Sitting uninstalled between two decrepit turbines were massive brand new air-conditioning units shipped all the way from York Corporation in Oklahoma. Pasted on one side of each unit was a glittering sticker proudly displaying the "Made in USA" sign, complete with the Stars and Stripes.

It's just what the Iraqis don't need at this time. Since May, Yaarub Jasim, general director for the southern region of Iraq's electricity ministry, has been pleading with Bechtel to deliver urgently needed spare parts for their antiquated turbines. "We asked Bechtel many times to please help us because the demand for power is very high and we should cover this demand," Jasim said. "We asked many times, many times."

Two weeks ago, Bechtel finally came through. Before it could deliver any of Jasim's requirements, however, Bechtel transported the air-conditioners, useless until the start of summer six months from now.

But even if the air-con units become eventually useful, emphasized plant manager Hamad Salem, other spare parts were much more important. The air-conditioners, Salem pointed out, were not even in the list of the equipment and machine components that they submitted to Bechtel.

A Monopoly on Iraq Reconstruction

Ideally, said Jasim, it would be best to get the spare parts from the companies that originally built the turbines because they would be more readily available and more suitable for their technology. Unfortunately, Jasim pointed out, Iraq's generators happened to have been provided by companies from France, Russia and Germany, the very countries banned by the Pentagon from getting contracts in Iraq, as well as Japan. On inspection, it was clear that the turbines don't carry the Stars and Stripes logo. The dilapidated turbines in Najibiya, for example, still bore "Made in USSR" plates.

Why then have the required components not been delivered? Jasim replied dismissively, as though the answer was self-evident: "Because no other company has been allowed by the US government, only Bechtel."

Unlike those among the other banned corporations, Bechtel carries the requisite brand. Since its founding, Bechtel's officials have had a long and very cozy relationship with and within the [United States government] now disbursing the billion-dollar contracts. For example, Bechtel board member George Schultz was former treasury secretary to Richard Nixon, secretary of state to Ronald Reagan, and coincidentally enough, chairman of the advisory board of the Committee for the Liberation of Iraq. Also once included on Bechtel's payroll were former Central Intelligence Agency chief John McCone, former defense secretary Casper Weinberger and former North Atlantic Treaty Organization supreme allied commander Jack Sheehan.

A Failure of International Proportions

Awaiting urgent rehabilitation, Iraq's French, Russian, German and Japanese-made power infrastructure is slowly disintegrating. At the station, workers are trying to make full use of the turbines by cooking pots of rice on the surface of the rusting hot pipes. If the stations are not rehabilitated any time soon, repairs will no longer be enough to keep them running, warned Jasim.

To finally end Iraq's crippling power shortage and to ensure that the turbines are not completely degraded, Bechtel should either quickly manufacture the required spare parts itself, a very long and very costly process, buy the spare parts from the Russian company directly, or hire the Russian firm as a sub-contractor. That, or they just allow the crumbling turbines to turn completely useless. Then they bid for building new billion-dollar power generators themselves.

Incidentally, part of Bechtel's contract includes making "road maps for future longer term needs and investments." In other words, Bechtel is currently being paid to determine what the Iraqis will "need" to buy in the future, using the Iraqi and US taxpayers' money. According to independent estimates, Bechtel stands to get up to 20 billion [dollars'] worth of reconstruction contracts in the next few years.

If Bechtel has grander plans for Iraq's power sector, however, their officers are not telling the Iraqis. The utilities managers interviewed said they are not being consulted at all regarding Iraq's strategic energy plans. Bechtel officials don't even bother to explain what's taking them so long to deliver the parts they need. "They just collect papers," said Jasim, head of Iraq's southern district oil ministry.

An Incentive to Fail

Iraq's power sector problem is illustrative of the bigger pattern. Iraqis spend up to five hours lining up for gasoline not only because of the sabotage of pipelines but also because there's limited electricity to run oil refineries that are crying for quicker action from Kellogg, Brown & Root (KBR), the Halliburton subsidiary and contractor for rehabilitating the oil infrastructure. According to workers from the South Oil Company in Basra, which KBR is obliged to rehabilitate, they are not aware of any repairs KBR has actually undertaken.

With Iraq's oil refineries still awaiting rehabilitation, Iraq cannot refine enough crude oil to meet domestic consumption. The US is instead exporting Iraq's crude oil and employing KBR under a no-bid cost-plus-fixed-fee contract to import gasoline from neighboring Turkey and Kuwait.

[A]n official Pentagon investigation [in 2003] revealed that KBR is charging the US government more than twice what others are paying for imported gasoline. What was left unsaid, however, is the conflict of interest inherent in hiring KBR for both the oil infrastructure reconstruction and the oil importation. If Iraq's pipelines and refineries were suddenly fully functional and Iraq was able to produce all the oil it needed, it would be the end of KBR's lucrative oil-importing business.

There has been no evidence that KBR is deliberately delaying the repair of the refineries, only that there is an obvious disincentive to speed things up. There is a serious but overlooked clash of incentives when the same company tasked to revive the oil industry is simultaneously making money from a condition in which that industry stays in tatters.

Squeezing the Iraqis

Just outside the Coalition Provisional Authority headquarters, a small unorganized group of employees of the former regime gathered and unfurled their banner. "We need our salaries now." They were demanding 10 months' worth of back wages. "We thank you because you saved our lives from Saddam. But we want to live so you should help us," their unofficial spokesperson Karim Hassin said indignantly, addressing the unresponsive 10-foot high wall protecting the compound. "Paul Bremer [CPA head] promised us salaries. We heard it with our own ears. What happened to these promises?"

A day after that the Pentagon's investigation on KBR was publicized, 300 soldiers walked out of the US-created 700-member New Iraqi Army, decrying unreasonably low wages. Most of the deserters were recruited from Saddam's former army, but for only $50 a month they had decided to transfer their allegiance to the occupation forces.

Trained by the military contractor Vinnell Corporation, their only demand from their new masters was a raise in pay to $120 a month. That would have amounted to a monthly increase in spending of only $49,000, small change beside the US's $4 billion monthly military spending in Iraq and a minuscule amount compared to the $61 million in overcharges by KBR, revealed by the Pentagon auditors.

Hearing about all these developments, it would appear that the occupation forces have come to liberate Iraq on a really tight budget. The common refrain of the Iraqis who have chosen to work with the US-installed bureaucracy is that there is no *quid pro quo* [a favor for a favor]. Pressed to explain the failure of his ministry to significantly increase power, for example, Iraq's electricity chief, Ayhem al-Samaraie, grudgingly admitted: "I have no money in my ministry at all."

Indeed, a quick visual survey of Baghdad from the dirty streets, the aging machines and the raging workers to the unbelievably long lines for gasoline, makes this explanation for Iraq's reconstruction problems sound almost convincing. That the reconstruction effort is in shambles because there is no money almost seems plausible.

None for Iraq, Billions for Bechtel

But it isn't. Last November, the US Congress eventually passed George W Bush's $87 billion request for Iraq with no fuss. Before that, the US had already spent $79 billion on both Iraq and Afghanistan. On top of this, the US also has complete control of the UN-authorized Development Fund for Iraq (DFI) which contains all of the former government's assets as well as past and future revenues from Iraq's oil exports, including leftover funds from the UN Oil for Food Program [from 1995 to 2003, it allowed Iraq to sell oil for food and medicine while under sanctions after the 1990–91 Gulf War].

By the end of the year, the DFI would have given the occupation forces access to a total of $10 billion in disposable funds. Though control would be less direct, the occupation forces can also tap a few more billions from the estimated $13 billion grants and loans raised during the Madrid donors' conference on Iraq [in] October [2002].

On paper, the amount that will be paid to contractors like Bechtel will come from US taxpayers' money. In practice, however, all that is being spent on Iraq's reconstruction is mixed in a pot containing the US's and other coalition-member countries' grants, plus the Iraqis' own funds.

So there's money; it's just not going around. And here perhaps lies the solution to the mystery of how the world's superpower and the world's biggest corporations can't even begin to put Iraq together again: The reconstruction is less about reconstruction than about making the most money possible.

[U.S.] [f]irms like Raytheon, Boeing and Northrop Grumman will get their fair share of the $4 billion that the US is spending monthly on military expenses in Iraq; but there will not be an extra dime for the New Iraqi Army recruits. Bechtel's useless Oklahoma-made air-conditioners will be paid for under the $680 million no-bid contract; but there will be no money for the sorely needed Russian-made components for Najibiya's turbines. Halliburton and its sub-contractors creamed off $61 million importing oil from Kuwait; but there will be no pay rise for Iraq's oil refinery workers.

While the US finds it increasingly hard to raise funds for the occupation, there is still enough money for the most critical aspects of the reconstruction. Those profiting from it, however, are determined to keep the biggest share possible to themselves. The bottom-line of the reconstruction mess is the bottom-line: little gets done because contractors cannot see beyond the dollar sign.

Profiting from Reconstruction

"The profit motive is what brings companies to dangerous locations. But that is what capitalism is all about," Richard Dowling, spokesperson of the US Army Corps of Engineers, the agency that contracted Kellogg, Brown & Root, explained. "If it takes profit to motivate an organization to take on a tough job, we can live with that. Yes, there's a profit motive but the result is the job gets done."

The problem is, as evidenced most clearly by the case of Bechtel and KBR, the job is not even getting half-done. Profit-maximization has not resulted in the most efficient restoration of power and oil production possible. On the contrary, it gets in the way of doing things right. The power plants will eventually be built and the oil refineries will run again, but not after unnecessary deprivation of the Iraqis and not after Bechtel has made the most of the opportunity.

This war to liberate Iraq was never about liberating the Iraqis. Unsurprisingly then, the reconstruction effort is also not about reconstruction. In this occupation, the US and its allies' primary goal is not to rebuild what they have destroyed; it's to make a fast buck. Contractors like Bechtel and KBR are assured of getting paid no matter what; that the power plants will eventually be constructed is just incidental. They will be built in order to justify the pretext for the profit-making: that a war had to be waged and that everything that was destroyed now has to be rebuilt.

As Stephen Bechtel, the company's founder, once made clear, "We are not in the construction and engineering business. We are in the business of making money." Billed as the biggest rebuilding effort since World War II, the reconstruction of Iraq is expected to cost $100 billion, some even say $200 billion [as of January 2007 the U.S. Inspector General for Iraq Reconstruction said the cost of the war and reconstruction has exceeded 300 billion dollars]. For the post-war contractors, this is not a reconstruction business; it is a hundred-billion-dollar bonanza.

"We'll Come Back with Weapons"

The US and its contractors are not even trying, for a simple reason: it's not the point. To assume that they are striving, but are merely failing because of factors beyond their control, is to presuppose that there is an earnest effort to succeed. There isn't. If there were, there should have been a coherent plan and process in which the welfare of the Iraqis—and not of the corporations—actually comes first. Instead, the Iraqis' need for electricity comes after Bechtel's need for billion-dollar projects. The Iraqis' need for decent living wages becomes relevant only after Halliburton has maximized its profits.

Indeed, if there were a sincere attempt to succeed, the US, as the responsible occupying power, should have had no qualms giving Iraqis what many emphatically say they need to finally make things work: the authority and the resources. "If only the money and spare parts were provided," electricity official Jasim said, "we could do a surgical operation." "If I'm going to do it without KBR, I can do it," said al-Khshab. "We have been doing this for the past 30 years without KBR. Give me the money and give me the proper authority and I'll do it." But the US won't because who knows what the Iraqis would do? Ask the Russians to repair their power plants? Actually succeed in reconstructing their country without the involvement of Bechtel and Halliburton?

The US taxpayers are not parting with billions of dollars of their hard-earned pay to give away to some lucky Russian firm. US and coalition soldiers are not sacrificing their lives to protect the wussy French. The US did not liberate Iraq in order to let the long disempowered Iraqis rebuild their own country.

As the reconstruction process continues to disillusion Iraqis, the myth that the US is here to help is also steadily collapsing. With no light, no gasoline and no paychecks, more and more Iraqis are no longer just cursing the darkness. "If you want to live in peace, Americans, give us our salary," warned Hassim, the Iraqi protesting at the gates of the Coalition Provisional Authority. "If you do not, next time we'll come back with weapons."

Periodical Bibliography

The following articles have been selected to supplement the diverse views presented in this chapter.

Stuart W. Bowen Jr. "Improper Obligations Using the Iraq Relief and Reconstruction Fund Audit Report," Special Inspector General for Iraq Reconstruction, January 30, 2007, www.sigir.mil.

Duncan Currie "The Sistani Paradox; Building a Democracy with the Ayatollahs We Have," *The Weekly Standard*, May 10, 2006, www.weeklystandard .com.

Michael Douglas "Want to Build a Nation in Iraq?" *Akron Beacon Journal*, June 4, 2006, www.ohio.com.

Investor's Business Daily "Winning the Peace," January 26, 2007, www.investors.com.

Iraq Oil Ministry "Smuggling Crude Oil and Oil Products," Office of the Inspector General, May 22, 2006, www.iraqrevenuewatch.org.

Antonia Juhasz "Are U.S. Corporations Going to 'Win' the Iraq War?" *GregPalast.com*, October 26, 2006, www.gregpalast.com.

Frederick Kagan "Choosing Victory: A Plan for Success in Iraq," American Enterprise Institute, January 5, 2007, www.aei.org.

David Rieff "What Went Wrong in Iraq?" *The New Republic*, April 17, 2006, www.tnr.com.

Joseph Morrison Skelly "Winning, One Student at a Time," *National Review Online*, November 2, 2005, www.nationalreview.com.

United States Agency for International Development (USAID) "Reconstruction Weekly Update," January 6, 2006, www.usaid.gov.

OPPOSING
VIEWPOINTS®
SERIES

CHAPTER 4

Can Nation-Building Succeed in the 21st Century?

Chapter Preface

Wall Street Journal columnist Bret Stephens wrote in the February 2007 issue of Commentary magazine: "[I]n the past 30 years, the pace of democratization around the world has been hugely speeded by the collapse of the Soviet Union, inexpensive mass-communications technologies, economic interdependence, and rising standards of living."

Stephens argues that the acceleration toward freedom and democracy has never been more rapid: "The more the practice of democracy has spread, the easier it has become for non-democratic societies to acquire it." Running for president in 2000, candidate George W. Bush famously proclaimed he did not want the U.S. Armed Forces nation-building around the globe. "I don't think our troops ought to be used for what's called nation building. . . . I mean, we're going to have some kind of nation-building corps from America? Absolutely not."

Six years later, during his second term, President George W. Bush has essentially created that corps in the form of a new State Department office called the Office of the Coordinator for Reconstruction and Stabilization (S/CRS). Many analysts cite the September 11, 2001 terrorist attacks on America and the Iraq occupation and nation-building mission as the reason for President Bush's reversal on foreign policy.

If nation-building is inevitable, can the United States, the United Nations, and allies build states that can succeed in the long run? Because the Iraq occupation and reconstruction has, as of this writing, been violent and difficult, it is hard to envision a functioning Iraq. Foreign policy analyst Ted Galen Carpenter has. He wrote in a 2004 article for Chronicles magazine: "With Washington's blessing, Iraq is building the same type of elephantine bureaucratic structure that is so typical of left-wing, Third World countries. . . . Many of these bureaucracies involve missions that are either unnecessary or could be performed far better by the private sector."

Carpenter's argument is an interesting claim: President George W. Bush, a conservative who denounced nation-building and claimed unqualified support of the free market during his election campaign, pledging to shrink big government, is elected president and converted into a bureaucratic expansionist who exports socialism in the form of nation-building. If the rest of the world is supposedly moving from a socialist-Communist ideology to embracing at least a minimum form of democracy to enjoin the global economy, how could President George W. Bush stray so far from his conservative roots?

One easy answer is that Carpenter is wrong. However, residents in the Middle East have a saying—"Every time there is a war, America learns geography." Exporting democratic values and nation-building through an American cultural lens may not work in the Middle East. If President Bush intends to let international forces become peacekeeping nation-builders to reduce American costs, as is the situation in Afghanistan as of 2007, the American agenda becomes tangled within the objectives of the United Nations and their offices, the International Security Assistance Force (ISAF) group, who supply personnel and equipment, and nongovernmental organizations (NGOs) from various countries. The goals that emerge from multi-organizational chains of command are lowest common denominator compromises that Carpenter terms "a system of politically correct welfare-state socialism."

Nation-building in complex failed states like Iraq, the Congo, Haiti, and Liberia cannot be done by any one nation alone. What if the central problem to nation-building success is that such massive undertakings require building a welfare-centric health and social service economy that is more European and pan-African, and thus more recognizable to the

Middle East, than American? Can that model be successful, and if so, would Americans continue to fund it?

The authors of the following viewpoints argue whether nation-building can succeed in the 21st century, what it might look like, how it might be achieved, or even if it should be attempted.

> *"Looking at the post-Iraq world, two re-*
> *alities jump out. In the United States,*
> *nation-building will be a dirty word.*
> *And, across the globe, nation-building*
> *will remain desperately necessary."*

Nation-Building Must Succeed in the 21st Century

Peter Beinart

In this viewpoint, Peter Beinart reveals how the Congo, often forgotten in a world consumed by violence in the Middle East, is one of the most wretched states on the planet. Using the Congo as an example, Beinart notes that Europe is preparing for more nation-building in the 21st century, while the United States seems prepared to diminish its role. Beinart argues that all nations, especially the United States, must establish nation-building as a viable strategy, or risk losing our moral status. Peter Beinart is an editor-at-large for The New Republic *magazine.*

As you read, consider the following questions:

1. What are the three main models for nation-building that were occurring in 2006, according to Beinart?

2. According to the author, what combination of forces might help broken states nation-build based on the Congo model?

3. What organization has the greatest expertise in global nation-building, according to Beinart?

In the world today, there are three models for how to save a country on the brink. The first is Iraq, where the United States—largely alone—is trying to prevent a dictatorship from sliding into chaos. The second is Afghanistan, where the United States is doing much the same thing with NATO support.

The third is almost invisible to Americans. It is the Congo, where the largest U.N. peacekeeping operation in the world is struggling to rescue one of the most wretched countries on earth. And it is doing so with virtually no high-level involvement by the United States.

The Congo makes Iraq and Afghanistan look prosperous. Seventy-five percent of the population is malnourished; 20 percent of children die before age five. In the 1950s, life expectancy was 55; today, it is 51.

A Dead Nation

During the cold war, when the West propped up anti-communist megalo-maniac Mobutu Sese Seko—for whom the term "kleptocrat" [plundering the country to gain personal wealth] was coined—many assumed that conditions in the Congo could not possibly get worse. They were wrong. In 1996, Rwanda and Uganda—angry at Mobutu for sheltering the Hutu militias that carried out the Rwandan genocide—helped replace him with rebel leader Laurent Kabila. But, as *The Economist*'s Kinshasa correspondent has noted, Kabila proved "equally brutal and corrupt, but less intelligent." While drunk, he sometimes ordered people executed, only to forget he had done so after sobering up.

In 1998, Kabila fell out with his Ugandan and Rwandan patrons, who sponsored a rebellion that nearly removed him from power. But Kabila turned to Angola and Zimbabwe, which saved his government in return for carte blanche to plunder its wealth. Soon, the Congo was a vast carcass, picked at by nine of its neighbors and countless local militias. In the civil war that raged until 2003, almost four million Congolese died—the largest death toll since World War II.

Enter the UN

Finally, after Laurent Kabila was assassinated and his son Joseph Kabila assumed power, most of the parties reached a peace deal, which the United Nations was brought in to enforce. At first, it did nothing of the sort. Peacekeepers watched as violence continued to ravage eastern portions of the country. One Congolese observer wondered if the blue helmets were "here to do anything apart from count the bodies."

But, a couple of years ago, the peacekeeping mission began stirring to life. It gained a savvy new head, replaced a hapless contingent of Uruguayans with more numerous—and more experienced—Indians, Pakistanis, and Bangladeshis, and moved aggressively into the Congo's lawless east. The European Union sent 2,000 of its own soldiers to help secure Kinshasa.

In 2006, in perhaps the greatest logistical accomplishment in electoral history, the Congo held its first free election in 40 years. In a country as big as western Europe, with only 500 kilometers of paved roads, the U.N. spearheaded an effort that registered 25 million people and established 50,000 polling places. The election was moderately fair, and turnout topped 80 percent. [In 2006], after a second-round runoff, the Congolese Supreme Court certified Kabila as the winner.

Only a fool would be sanguine about the Congo's future. Kabila, while better than his father, is hardly a democrat. His main rival, Jean-Pierre Bemba—who wields his own private

Securing Recovery

[T]he modest UN peacekeeping force sent to Mozambique in 1992 set the stage for Mozambique's recovery from a brutal civil war and for the remarkable economic boom that followed. In fact, soldiers with guns are sometimes the most effective form of foreign aid. In Chad, right now, it doesn't make sense to build clinics or train midwives since the Sudanese-financed janjaweed militia is storming through Darfur and Chad, slaughtering people because of their tribe or skin color. What Chadians need most is a small protection force to stop the genocidal marauders so that they can't butcher children in schools or burn down clinics.

Nicholas D. Kristof, "Aid: Can It Work?"
New York Review of Books, *October 5, 2006. www.nybooks.com.*

security force—could still violently contest the result. The election revealed a country split along tribal and linguistic lines. And the Congolese state isn't merely corrupt and brutal; as a provider of basic services, it barely exists.

A Coalition of Hope

But, nonetheless, the Congo hasn't been this hopeful since the 1960s. And the credit goes to an intriguing coalition of European money, African diplomacy, South Asian muscle, and U.N. expertise. Although U.N. formulas require the United States and Japan to foot a significant share of any peacekeeping bill, it was mostly the Europeans who financed the elections. South Africa and Angola pressured Kabila and Bemba to respect the results. South Asian troops kept the peace.

As the United States grows allergic to nation-building in the wake of Iraq, some combination of these forces might be the world's best hope for nursing broken nations back to health. While Europeans are more reluctant to wage war than Americans, they are often more inclined to help keep the peace. In fact, the European Union is developing a 60,000-person rapid-reaction force largely for that purpose. South Asia has become the world's largest source of peacekeepers, and the numbers could grow as India flexes its international muscle.

Then there's the United Nations itself—which, while often mocked in the United States (sometimes deservedly), has become the foremost repository of peacekeeping expertise in the world. As RAND's [analyst] James Dobbins has pointed out, both the United States and the United Nations did a lot of postwar stabilization in the '90s. But, while the Bush administration essentially discarded that knowledge and started from scratch in Afghanistan and Iraq, the United Nations now has a cadre of officials with extensive nation-building experience. Of course, Turtle Bay [New York site of the United Nations] can't overthrow governments. But, when it comes to ushering post-conflict societies toward democracy and peace, as Dobbins notes, the United Nations actually has a better record than the United States.

Nation-Building: A Desperate Necessity

Looking at the post-Iraq world, two realities jump out. In the United States, nation-building will be a dirty word. And, across the globe, nation-building will remain desperately necessary. As Oxford University [economists] Paul Collier and Anke Hoeffler have shown, peacekeeping is the most cost-effective way to prevent a country from sliding back into chaos. Indeed, the rise of international peacekeeping deserves significant credit for the decline in civilian deaths since the end of the cold war.

If the United States no longer has much appetite for such endeavors, we should at least support those who do. Largely as a result of the Congo, U.N. peacekeeping costs have shot up, and it is easy to imagine the United States trying to rein them in. We should do exactly the reverse. To consolidate its fledging democracy, the Congo actually needs more blue helmets—and we should help pay for them. The United States goes through missionary phases and anti-missionary phases, but, in the end, this isn't really about us. The important thing isn't who saves countries like the Congo; it is that they get saved.

> *"The real lesson of [nation-building in] Bosnia is that the creation of a peaceful multiethnic state with a strong central government is a dangerous mirage."*

Nation-Building Does Not Need to Succeed in the 21st Century

Ivan Eland

Ivan Eland is director of the Center on Peace and Liberty at the Independent Institute and author of The Emperor Has No Clothes: U.S. Foreign Policy Exposed. *Eland argues in this viewpoint that the United States continually celebrates nation-building in Bosnia but an examination of the results reveals inherent weaknesses in the Bosnia state-building plan. He further points out that the Iraq reconstruction falls somewhere between America's involvement in Vietnam and Bosnia, with differing, but mainly negative results.*

As you read, consider the following questions:

1. According to Eland, U.S. interventionist policy-makers would like to take the lessons of Bosnian nation-building and use them where?

2. If Bosnian nation-building is a failure, according to the author, why has the inter-ethnic violence in Bosnia almost completely stopped?

3. Do the ethnic and religious groups in Bosnia and Iraq want to live together, according to Eland?

The State Department [used] a 10-year anniversary party celebrating the Dayton accords [a peace treaty signed in 1995, ending 3 1/2 years of fighting between Serbia, Croatia, and Bosnia] to make more "progress" on Bosnia's future. The reality is that the interventionist U.S. foreign policy elite, led by the Bush administration's Undersecretary of State, Nicholas Burns, [hosted] the conclave of Bosnian leaders in Washington [in November 2005] to "fix" the Bosnian constitution enshrined by the Dayton accords. The elite want to create a strong central government and abolish the rotating presidency in favor of a national president and two vice presidents. This plan is only likely to make the still precarious situation in Bosnia deteriorate. Even worse, these interventionists would like to take lessons from the failed attempt at nation-building in Bosnia and use them to attempt to remedy the desperate situation in Iraq.

After the U.S. suffered a bloody nose in Vietnam, U.S. interventionism temporarily fell out of favor. The U.S. foreign policy elite—who see the globe as a giant chessboard and who don't mind sending other peoples' sons and daughters to die in faraway brushfire wars that have little to do with actually defending the United States—derisively called this "casualty aversion." As [U.S.] casualties in Vietnam rose, the American public rightly became suspicious of the interventionists' pet projects abroad.

Bosnia: Nothing to Brag About

The elite, while vociferously disavowing any similarities between Vietnam and Iraq, are deathly afraid that a similar prudent public casualty aversion caused by a failure in the Iraq

A Disgrace of Nation-Building

What can now be said about the American "success" in nation building? With the turmoil in Iraq, the advocates of U.S. intervention there admit it may take decades to bring democracy to that nation, as if time were the crucial ingredient. It has now been 106 years since the United States intervened in the Philippine Islands—how does economic development and democracy there measure up to American promises?

The *Asia Times* has recently published a lengthy editorial and five-part series, "The Philippines: Disgraceful State," by Pepe Escobar. The series completely disputes the neocons' revisionist history, revealing the utter *failure* of the U.S. intervention in the Philippines over the last century. As in Iraq, the results in the Philippines have been an enormous loss of life, extremely poor economic development, massive political corruption and human rights abuses, and a political system hardly embodying self-determination, let alone democracy.

William Marina, *"The Three Stooges in Iraq,"* Newsroom, *The Independent Institute, October 14, 2004, www.independent.org.*

war will affect public support for future military social engineering abroad. So they are grasping at the Bosnian straw to pull themselves out of the Iraq mess. In the sparse universe of successful nation-building by outside foreign powers, Bosnia may be the best recent example, but is certainly nothing to brag about.

Ten years after the Dayton accords, NATO peacekeepers are still on the scene and all parties agree that they will be needed for years to come. What this state of affairs really means is that if the outside peacekeepers departed, the Bosnian civil war would probably reignite. The lethargic maturing of the Bosnian police and army shows that the Bush administration's claim of rapid progress in training Iraqi security forces should be taken with a grain of salt. In fact, in a [2005] article in *The Atlantic Monthly*, journalist James Fallows notes that the Iraqi insurgency is worsening faster than the Iraqi security forces are improving.

Further uncomfortable similarities between Bosnia and Iraq exist. For example, the U.S. dumped billions of dollars into the reconstruction of the Bosnian economy and slathered U.S. taxpayer money on Iraq. Bosnia is certainly not an example of government-driven post-war economic recovery, and prospects for the same in Iraq are equally dismal. The efficacy of U.S. aid is even more questionable in Iraq because it has arrived while the fighting is still going on.

Also, NATO forces in Bosnia have been unable (or unwilling) to capture the Bosnian Serb war criminals Radovan Karadzic and Ratko Mladic. Similarly, U.S. forces have had difficulty capturing or killing Abu Musab al-Zarqawi, the leader of al Qaeda forces in Iraq [al-Zarqawi was killed by the United States in June 2006].

What Prevents a Return to Civil War?

The only thing that can be said for the Dayton accords is that they have stopped the fighting in Bosnia for a time. The U.S. foreign policy establishment, however, has attributed this lull in carnage to U.S. military and political pressure, as well as to the presence of NATO peacekeepers during the ensuing 10 years. Actually, it probably has more to do with the decentralization of government in this multi-ethnic state. The Dayton accords created Serb and Muslim-Croat mini-states and a weak national government. Columnist Jackson Diehl, an interventionist, disparages such decentralization by calling it a "deeply flawed plan for federalism." He bemoans the three-member presidency, which rotates between Serbs, Croats and Muslims, as well as the existence of 14 education ministries and 15 police agencies.

Yet because the central government is weak, the various ethnic groups have less fear that one group—such as the Serbs in the former Yugoslavia—could get control of the levers of power and oppress or murder the other groups. Although Bosnia has an uneasy peace, this decentralization probably at least somewhat inhibits the return to civil war.

The Real Lesson of Bosnia

But the lesson that the interventionists take from the Bosnian experience is that intensive diplomacy by a unified Western coalition, enough troops on the ground (Bosnia initially had more than twice the number of foreign troops per capita as stationed in Iraq), and resistance to the temptation to pull them out can achieve success in building a strong multi-ethnic national government.

Instead, the real lesson of Bosnia is that the creation of a peaceful multiethnic state with a strong central government is a dangerous mirage. Holding together an artificial state with ethnic or religious cleavages using foreign military power is unlikely to be successful anywhere. Decentralization in both Bosnia and Iraq is the only hope for peace and prosperity. The ethnic or religious groups in neither country really want to live together. In both countries, the United States should stop its risky attempts to create a strong national government and allow genuine self-determination. In Iraq, this might take the form of a loose confederation or partition, with a sharing of petroleum revenues or oil fields to entice Sunni participation.

> *"Regenerative power turns nation building on its head. Rather than imposing a blueprint from outside, participants respond to the needs of the affected community."*

Small Projects Contribute to Nation-Building

Jason M. Brownlee

Jason M. Brownlee argues in this viewpoint that typical nation-building fails because it does not recognize indigenous needs and cultures; instead, Western reconstruction models tend to create instability. He argues for a new version that does not attempt state building or coercion through military occupation, but relies on regenerative, organic constructions based on localized needs. Jason M. Brownlee is a former postdoctoral scholar at the Center on Democracy, Development and the Rule of Law.

As you read, consider the following questions:

1. According to Brownlee, when has the United States performed nation-building most poorly?

2. "Regenerative" nation-building is limited in scope because it relies on what, according to Brownlee?

Jason M. Brownlee, "Why Nation-Building Is a Known Unknowable," *CDDRL News*, Center on Democracy, Development, and the Rule of Law, Stanford University, January 8, 2005. http://cddrl.stanford.edu. Reproduced by permission.

3. A key mistake of foreign and occupying nation-builders has been their reliance upon what, according to the viewpoint author?

As the conflict In Iraq reminds us, nation building confounds its architects' designs with almost predictable regularity. Investments of time, resources, and specialized knowledge have not enabled large-scale political engineering. Instead, would-be nation builders have been frustrated by a proliferation of unintended consequences and their inability to elicit societal participation in their projects. Results depend more upon initial conditions prior to an intervention than the nation builder's exertions upon arrival.

Hence, the U.S. has performed most poorly when its mission required the most work (e.g., Somalia, Haiti, Iraq). Conversely, it has done best where it did less (Germany, Japan), deferring to old-regime civil servants and upgrading already functional institutions. Given the humbling record of Western powers at navigating the perils of macro-level political planning, the "how" of nation-building should be considered, in the formulation of [former U.S.] Defense Secretary Donald Rumsfeld, a known unknown.

Large-Scale Nation-Building Doesn't Work

More likely, it is a known unknowable. The extent or unintended consequences and contingency in largescale political engineering makes disappointment certain and disaster likely.

Twentieth-century experiences belie the notion that nation-building successes will solve the problem of state failures. Forces trying to impose regime change and raise new state structures immediately grapple with societal inertia and their own deficit in understanding local politics.

This dilemma pushes would-be nation builders down one of two undesirable paths. Either they recognize their inability to restructure indigenous political arrangements or they attempt to do so in vain. Despite plans of change at the outset of nation building, those executing the project soon embrace a change of plans.

Thus, even the most committed states have been hampered by an inability to develop political capacity on the ground and improve upon the initial endowments of the country being occupied. Institutional value-added has been minimal, reflecting the problem of state instability back upon those who expected to solve it.

These patterns raise serious doubts about the chances of success in even the most well-intentioned of regime change missions. They demarcate the limits of projecting state power abroad, whether for humanitarian or security purposes. The failures of imposed regime change lead to the conclusion that indigenous gradual political development—with all of its potential for authoritarianism and civil unrest—may be the optimal path for sustainable democratization and state building.

A Poor Record Using Past Lessons

When comparing the uneven history [of] post-colonial development with the poor record of nation building we are left paraphrasing Churchill's endorsement of democracy as the worst kind of government except for the alternatives: Sovereign political development may be the worst form of government except for all those kinds of nation building that have been tried.

Infrastructural weakness is not a technical problem surmountable through systematic review of prior experiences. Indeed, the notion of "learning past lessons" deceptively implies that the current generation of academics and policymakers can succeed where their predecessors failed. The idea that nation building is a flawed but salvageable project prejudges its fundamental viability.

Betting on the Small Nation-Builders

The nation-builders to bet on are those refugee families piled onto the brightly painted Pakistani truck moving up the dusty roads, the children perched on the mattresses, like Mowgli astride the head of an elephant, gazing toward home.

The nation-builders to invest in are the teachers, especially the women who taught girls in secret during the Taliban years. I met one in an open-air school right in the middle of Kabul's most destroyed neighborhood. She wrote her name in a firm, bold hand in my notebook, and she knew exactly what she needed: chalk, blackboards, desks, a roof and, God willing, a generation of peace. At her feet, on squares of U.N.H.C.R. [United Nations High Commission for Refugees] sheeting, sat her class, 20 upturned faces, all female, having the first reading lesson of their lives.

Michael Ignatieff, "Nation-Building Lite,"
New York Times Magazine, *July 28, 2002. www.nytimes.com.*

A Third Way of Nation-Building

Once we have set our sights on rescuing an enterprise that has repeatedly frustrated its architects and their subjects, we screen out alternatives that more effectively serve the same development goals. We also risk funneling research down an intellectual cul-de-sac, at great cost in time, resources, and lives lost for those participating in failed regime-change missions. Therefore, a more productive direction for contemporary interest in nation building may mean backing up and reassessing the core problem of weak states, on one hand, and the limits of foreign intervention, on the other. Ensuring a positive impact on the country considered for intervention requires orienting the enterprise away from the takeover of state functions and toward the short-term provision of aid to local communities.

Apart from the futile pursuit of infrastructural power or the doomed deployment of despotic power (coercion), one can envision a third kind of influence, "regenerative power," which is exercised during relief efforts, such as emergency assistance following natural disasters.

Regenerative power involves neither the adoption of domestic state functions nor physical coercion. It denotes the ability of a state to develop infrastructure under the direction of the local population. For example, it means rebuilding a post office, but not delivering the mail. It is typified by the U.S. response to natural disaster relief within its own borders and abroad.

Limiting Scale, Gaining Power

Regenerative power turns nation building on its head. Rather than imposing a blueprint from outside, participants respond to the needs of the affected community. It is restorative rather than transformative. There is no preexisting master plan for what the "final product" will be, but rather an organically evolving process in which the assisting group serves at the direction of the people being assisted.

The exercise of regenerative power is inherently limited in scale since it depends on local engagement rather than elite planning. It is inimical to macro-level ambitions but it also acquires a bounded effectiveness that imposed regime change lacks. Where nation building attempts to overwrite existing organization and only belatedly incorporates local understanding, disaster relief efforts and regenerative projects begin from the assumption that local communities know best their own needs. Existing social networks and patterns of authority are an asset, not a hindrance, and local know-how offers the principal tool for resolving local crises.

Rather than pursuing the often destructive delusion of interventionist state transformation, regenerative power starts from an interest in using state power for constructive purposes and a sober assessment of the limits of that aim. The assisting foreign groups serve under the direction of indigenous political leaders toward the achievement of physical reconstruction and emergency service provision.

With remarkable prescience Rumsfeld commented in October 2001, "I don't know people who are smart enough from other countries to tell other countries the kind of arrangements they ought to have to govern themselves."

Engaging Uncertainty

The experience of twentieth century U.S. interventions and ongoing operations in Iraq [as of this writing] supports his insight. Proponents of nation building or shared sovereignty arrangements have exaggerated the ability of powerful states to foster institutions in developing countries. The empirical record, from successful outcomes in Germany and Japan to dismal failures across the global south, shows the societies alleged to be most in need of strong institutions have proven the least tractable for foreign administration. Rather than transmitting new modes of organization, would-be nation builders have relied upon existing structures for governance.

This dependence on the very context that was intended for change reveals how little infrastructural power nation builders wield. They are consistently unable to implement political decisions through the local groups. Contrary to recent arguments that sustained effort and area expertise can enable success, nation building has foundered despite such investments.

Understanding that nation building is a "known unknowable" is crucial for redirecting intervention where it can be more effective. Advocates of humanitarian assistance should consider the merits of smaller, regenerative projects that can respond better to uncertainty and avoid the perils of large-scale political engineering.

| "It remains a dubious proposition that both Afghanistan and Iraq can be shaped into fully functioning and integrated (within the globalized economic infrastructure) nation-states."

Ethnic Diversity Prohibits Nation-Building

Matthew Riemer

Matthew Riemer argues in this viewpoint that nation-building, by the United States and large Western powers, transforms into chaos due to the minority interests of varying factions and warlords in states where there is no unified philosophy of culture and governance. Though the United States is against nation-state fragmentation, that is exactly what it produces, to the detriment of the majority populations in those countries. Matthew Riemer is a Russian expert and editor and columnist for yellow times.org.

As you read, consider the following questions:

1. Riemer states that the United States is uncovering a troublesome truth in its global attempts at nation-building. What is that truth?

Matthew Riemer, "Post-War Patterns in Afghanistan and Iraq," *Power and Interest News Report*, August 12, 2003. Reproduced by permission.

2. Why do world leaders not want Iraq and other violent nations to divide into independent states, according to the viewpoint author?

3. What should the United States understand if it truly seeks democracy in volatile regions around the world, according to Riemer?

Though the wars fought in Afghanistan [2001] and Iraq [2003] were tactically dissimilar and of varying levels of intensity, the post-war social, cultural, and political factors at play are very similar. The most relevant and foundational similarity between the two countries is their creation: each was cobbled together from amongst a plethora of local, autonomous/tribal regions into reluctant wholes in the form of what the conquering country felt to be a modern nation-state. And for both, since their involuntary birth, this fact has hampered their development, as well as posing a deep, historical puzzle for, first, Great Britain and, now, the United States, in their efforts at "nation building."

This predicament—if only in the name of thoroughness—must eventually elicit a series of important questions from the concerned observer, some of which might be:

- What are the inherent weaknesses of the "nation-state" model?

- When Washington uses the phrase "nation building," what does this really imply?

- Is the so-called "nation-state" a viable model for Afghanistan and Iraq?

The Troublesome Truth of Ethnic Diversity

The United States may be uncovering a troublesome truth in its latest global endeavors: the fact that the nation-state is not a universal model for all regions and peoples of the world, and, in some cases, it may even obstruct the development of

Signe Wilkinson Editorial Cartoon © 2002 Signe Wilkinson. Used with the permission of Signe Wilkinson and the Washington Post Writers Group in conjunction with the Cartoonist Group.

the very stability and select economic development the U.S. is seeking through its operations—especially in areas with a concentration of ethnic diversity like in the Balkans, the Caucasus, and much of Central Asia where state-sized regions more readily stabilize under a sub-network of autonomous zones defined by some obvious feature, whether it be ethnic, linguistic, or geographical.

The dominant U.S. polity has always assumed that the keys to American success are the keys to global success, that what works for them will work for others. This belief has led many in the U.S. leadership to think that concepts like democracy and free market capitalism can be smoothly exported to other regions and environments and have the same effect that they had in 18th and 19th century America. This widely held belief is shared by the Bush administration and has been explicitly stated in its 2002 National Security Strategy.

An Economy of the Founding Fathers

However, unlike modern day Afghanistan and Iraq, America, at the time of its founding, consisted of a single ruling class that came together to codify the social and economic rules that others would live by and best continue their prosperity. These individuals were all wealthy, Caucasian, Christian males who shared broad and overlapping interests. These-so-called "founding fathers" [writers of the Constitution and Declaration of Independence] also decided upon their inherent and inevitable sovereignty and its announcement at a time and place of their choosing.

This picture, to even the most casual of observers, paints a perfect contrast with the countries the U.S. is currently attempting nation building in today. Both countries represent a diverse array of languages, religions, and cultural traditions, while encompassing regions that were never unified in the sense that a modern day independent state is. This fact alone complicates the democratic process to the point of futility: the biggest obstacle being the interests of minority groups within any given state.

But this is a painful reality for Washington to accept as it greatly affects the continuation of economic paradigms so cherished throughout the centers of power in the Western world. If the Bush administration, other influential world leaders, and future U.S. administrations were to accept a greater amount of regional autonomy in distant lands—like by letting Iraq splinter into three independent states or at least autonomous regions—this would greatly affect the implementation of laws concerning free trade and deregulation; such political forms provide infrastructural barriers to the rather organic growth of free market economies. By being self-contained and, to a certain degree, self-reliant, regions where such a process were to take place inhibit the plans of Washington's economists.

Shifting the Balance of Power

There are other concerns, however, when hypothetically imagining the break-up of larger states into multiple smaller ones.

One of the biggest of these fears is the potential shift in regional power balances. For example, if southern Iraq were to become its own state completely dominated by Shi'ittes, this would undoubtedly portend some kind of union with Iran possibly to the point of annexation on the part of Tehran [capital of Iran]. If the Kurds [indigenous ethnic group who consider themselves part of an autonomous nation called Kurdistan] in the north [of Iraq] were to gain their independence this would ruffle Turkey and put diplomatic pressure on Washington. This is obviously not in the interests of the United States.

Further east in Central Asia, reflections on Afghanistan produce similar results. Afghanistan is different from Iraq in that it has endured failed government after failed government for decades with regular periods of anarchy—warlords unconvincingly filling the power vacuums—while Iraq was ruled consistently by [dictator Saddam Hussein's] centralized power. If Afghanistan were to fragment it would be more difficult to predict what may happen—virtually all the warlords have both fought and been allied with one another at some point. Certainly the border between Afghanistan and Pakistan in the south and east would completely blur if the Pashtuns [ethnic group primarily in east and south Afghanistan, and north and west Pakistan] were to realize a long-awaited Pashtunistan; in the eyes of Washington, this would provide an undesirable strategic boost for Islamabad [Pakistan's capital] despite their partnership in the U.S. "war on terrorism." And, like in Iraq, Iran could be expected to curry favor with those along its border—Iranian border patrols did skirmish with the Taliban from time to time—such as the governor of Herat [city in western Afghanistan], Ismail Khan.

Because of such potential for unpredictable and dangerous events, such state fragmentation will remain a non-starter for Washington—market growth, acquisition, and stability are just too at risk in that kind of environment.

Unlikely Nation-Building

So in this categorical rejection of new, or perhaps old, political forms, the United States must realize what that rejection brings to the table: the situation currently faced by the occupying forces in both Afghanistan and Iraq today. In both countries, diverse groups with less overlapping agendas than more are jockeying for position in a post-war context that features low-intensity guerrilla warfare, an occupying army, and the marginalization of large percentages of the population.

It remains a dubious proposition that both Afghanistan and Iraq can be shaped into fully functioning and integrated (within the globalized economic infrastructure) nation-states capable of long periods of stability, relative peace, and economic growth.

Democracy Does Not Equal Stability

The United States must decide what it really wants. Does it want democracy? And if it does, it must realize what democracy can actually mean in volatile regions such as Afghanistan and Iraq. Instability and democracy are not mutually exclusive conditions—democracy does not equal stability—and revolution—regardless of what one conceives it to be—is a democratic expression. Given a true choice, many people in many countries may feel no solidarity with a colonially created "nation."

And if the primary interests of the United States are ones of economic security through expanded markets in new regions, the leadership in Washington must expect the degree of resistance to its efforts that it is now receiving in Eurasia.

> *"We as a nation have ample experience, gleaned from previous nation-building commitments, to plan and implement the necessary effort in Haiti."*

Nation-Building Is the Only Hope for Failed States

Jeffrey H. Fargo

Jeffrey H. Fargo, in this viewpoint, calls Haiti a "failed state" and discusses why previous nation-building efforts in Haiti have fallen apart. He argues that democratic expansionism should not be limited to the Middle East and that a failing Haiti is a humanitarian and security risk to the United States. He then describes how the mission might be accomplished in light of past history and nation-building partnerships. Jeffrey H. Fargo was a national security affairs fellow at the Hoover Institute from 2002-2003.

As you read, consider the following questions:

1. According to Fargo, what is needed to help Haiti become a member of the international community of legitimate nations again?

2. How does Fargo define failed states?

3. What organizations are critical to humanitarian relief and nation-building efforts globally, according to the author?

On February 29, 2004, following a three-week uprising in which Haitian rebels seized control of the central and northern portions of the country and threatened to seize the capital, Port-au-Prince, President Jean-Bertrand Aristide resigned his office and left the country for temporary asylum in the Central African Republic. (Aristide ultimately took exile in South Africa in late May [2004].)

In the wake of Aristide's departure, an international peacekeeping force, made up of 3,600 troops from the United States, Canada, Chile, and France, partially restored stability to the island nation, but the rebels still controlled much of the rural area when the transition to the U.N. peacekeeping force occurred on June 1 [2004]. Less than 10 years had passed since the last United States–led intervention, Operation Uphold Democracy, in September 1994, which restored the democratically elected President Aristide to power and deposed the military junta that had ousted him by coup in 1991. This is the third U.S. intervention in less than a century (the United States also occupied Haiti from 1915 until 1934).

A Long-Term Effort Is Needed

Haiti is widely recognized as a failed state. Many would question whether we should engage in nation building on the island, considering our previous efforts there and the country's lack of progress despite periodic infusions of foreign aid. Nation building became part of our foreign policy under the Clinton administration, with its interventions in Somalia, Bosnia, and Haiti. The Bush administration came into office opposed to nation building, but after 9/11, the U.S. invasions of both Afghanistan [2001] and Iraq [2003] have resulted in long-term commitments to nation building. Thus, we as a nation have ample experience, gleaned from previous nation-building commitments, to plan and implement the necessary effort in Haiti.

What is needed to assist Haiti to rejoin the international community of legitimate nation-states and for it to comply with international norms? The experience of the United States and the international community in assisting Haiti from 1994 to 2001 clearly shows that more is needed than a short-term humanitarian response or crisis management effort. To be successful, the United States and the international community will have to commit to a long-term political, socioeconomic, and security development plan. This will require political will, a flexible time line, and a long-term commitment of resources to assist Haiti in reestablishing democracy and conducting itself as a sovereign state, able to respond to its responsibilities to both its own people and the international community. If this type of long-term effort is not implemented to foster the growth of its political and socioeconomic institutions, then Haiti will continue to fail and will periodically present the United States and the international community with the necessity of intervention and costly humanitarian assistance and peacekeeping operations.

Reasons for Nation Building in Haiti

Although at the time of this writing [in 2004] the United States was planning to withdraw its forces from Haiti by the end of June [2004], it would be in our national security interests to fully support a new long-term nation-building commitment in Haiti and to use our influence to win the support of other nations and international organizations to participate in this desperately needed assistance. There are several reasons. First, America is about values, and current U.S. foreign policy advocates promoting freedom and democracy abroad. It would be a travesty to limit our efforts in this regard to the Middle East, or other regions, and to ignore a failed democracy in America's own backyard. Second, Haiti is a humanitarian crisis that we cannot afford to ignore, especially with close to one million Haitians living in the United States. Finally, Haiti is a failed state, which brings with it serious threats and negative consequences for U.S. national security, particularly because of its proximity to America's borders.

Although some Americans may disagree with promoting democracy and freedom abroad, it is currently the foreign policy of the Bush administration. President Bush, in his preface to the *United States National Security Strategy*, published in 2002, clearly states the U.S. commitment to promoting freedom and democracy globally: "We will actively work to bring the hope of democracy, development, free markets, and free trade to every corner of the world." Events in Afghanistan and Iraq, and Bush administration statements related to the U.S. nation-building efforts in those countries, have clearly established U.S. foreign policy in this regard.

The Results of Undemocratic Governments

During its 200 years of independence, Haiti has undergone a long and tortured history of undemocratic changes of government, mostly through violent coups. The election of Jean-Bertrand Aristide as president in 1990 was seen as the first free and fair democratic election in Haiti's history. His populist orientation and new political party, Lavalas Family, gave many hopes of a government that would benefit the Haitian poor, instead of exploiting them, as has been the long-established norm. However, in 1991, the Haitian military conducted a coup and Aristide was forced into exile in the United States. Finally, after much negotiation and years of sanctions, a U.S.–led intervention in 1994 forced out Haiti's military rulers and restored Aristide to power to complete the remainder of his five-year term.

At the insistence of the United States, Aristide was not allowed to run for president in 1995. Thus, his protégé and former prime minister, Rene Preval, was elected and served as president from 1995 to 2000, when Aristide was elected again. Unfortunately, the period of 1995 through 2004 was marked by ineffective governance, rife with fraudulent elections, political violence, corruption, and a refusal to privatize state-run industries. Instead of consolidating democratic institutions with the help of the United States and the international community, both the Preval and the Aristide administrations moved toward authoritarian rule, maintained a political stalemate with the opposition and the legislature, and failed to meet the international community's conditions for economic aid.

This political stalemate came to a head in February of [2004], when three years into Aristide's second five-year term, the political opposition demanded Aristide's resignation as a condition of any solution to Haiti's political impasse. Worsening living conditions in Haiti and disenchantment with Aristide had led to demonstrations and violence, including some deaths, since September 2003. The civil unrest and political impasse led to new negotiations by the Caribbean Community and Common Market (Caricom), of which Haiti is a member. The instability in Haiti was a regional concern, and organizations such as Caricom and the Organization of American States (OAS) attempted to help Haiti resolve its internal conflict before it reached the stage of widespread violence or regime change.

The erosion of democracy in Haiti is illustrated by the results of the Freedom House [organization supporting global freedom, mainly funded by the U.S. government] annual global assessment of the status of political rights and civil liberties. Its assessment of Haiti from 1994 through 2003 shows a downward trend due to political warfare, rampant corruption, and generalized social and political violence; it characterized Haiti from the year 2000 onward as "not free." The well-known nongovernmental organization Transparency International's

Success in El Salvador

[T]he Cold War featured a similarly successful, if smaller-scale, nation building. In the late 1980s, for instance, El Salvador was a bloody basket case, riven by a civil war and saddled with a corrupt and nasty government.

The United States, together with the United Nations, brokered the end of the fighting, and in so doing dictated in very specific terms the shape of the country's future political-civil life, from elections, to the composition of the police force, to the working of its judiciary.

Rich Lowry, "Two Cheers for Nation-Building,"
National Review *online, October 22, 2001. www.nationalreview.com.*

Corruptions Perceptions Index for 2003 listed Haiti as the most corrupt country in the Western Hemisphere.

The Poverty of Corruption

Humanitarian assistance programs from the United States, the United Nations, and various nongovernmental organizations (NGOs) were already addressing the widespread poverty and lack of basic services in Haiti before the February [2004] rebellion. However, the February armed uprising disrupted the economy, damaged the infrastructure, and caused looting of food and other supplies stored in warehouses at the ports. This exacerbated the already marginal situation and caused an enormous humanitarian crisis. There is a continuing lack of security in rural regions of Haiti that is still disrupting market activities and distribution of food aid and other types of humanitarian assistance. In response to the humanitarian crisis, which is estimated to seriously affect three million people of Haiti's total population of eight million, the United Nations has urgently appealed to its members for $35 million for emergency humanitarian aid to use for Haiti during the next six months. Unfortunately, the international community has been slow to respond and only a fraction of the $35 million has been donated. Haiti's interim prime minister [Boniface Alexandre] [was] discouraged by the fact the U.N. peacekeeping mandate [was] only for six months and attempt[ed] to get it extended until February 7, 2006, when newly elected president [Rene Preval] [was] inaugurated.

Haiti is the least developed country in the Western Hemisphere, one of the poorest countries in the world, and stands 150th of 175 countries ranked by the United Nations in its Human Development Index. Electricity is scarce to nonexistent because the national electric company and private contractors are unable or refuse to produce electricity until the government of Haiti pays its bills, which are in arrears. Many rural towns only receive potable water for two hours a day every few days or even less often. Infectious diseases and HIV/AIDS are significant and growing. The heavy reliance on charcoal for fuel has caused severe deforestation, leading to erosion and flooding. Tragedy struck again at the end of May [2004] when heavy rains caused flooding and mudslides that killed 1,600 people, destroyed hundreds of homes, and left hundreds missing.

Human capital has been badly neglected, as evidenced by a literacy rate of only 50 percent and a 90 percent reliance on private schools for primary education. The costs of paying for education, and the current economic hardships, have reduced the number of children in school. Many Haitians depend on remittances from abroad—mostly from Haitian relatives and friends living in the United States—to get by. These remittances, estimated at $800 million per year, are a critical component of the Haitian economy. Socioeconomic progress declined during the sanctions and embargo of the military junta years, 1991 to 1994, and Haiti's political instability and refusal to open the economy since then have meant that the population has never recovered economically. Thus, Haiti's per capita [per person] GDP [gross domestic product] of $425 is by far the lowest in the Americas; life expectancy for Haitians is only 49 years.

The United States cannot in good conscience turn its back on this disaster. To do so would undermine U.S. credibility and would expose U.S. foreign policy to accusations of racism, as has been alleged by the [U.S.] Congressional Black Caucus and others.

The Threat of Failed States

Failed states are countries in which the central government does not exert effective control over, or is unable to deliver vital services to, significant parts of its own territory due to conflict, ineffective governance, or state collapse. Haiti certainly fits this category: Since February 2004, the rebels, not the central government, have controlled larger and larger portions of the national territory. And even before the February conflict, the central government had been unable to provide such vital services as food, water, disease control, education, and security to the majority of the populace. Such failed states threaten U.S. national security interests by being safe havens for transnational threats, encouraging mass migration, destabilizing the region, spreading infectious disease, and bearing the unexpected costs of humanitarian assistance and peacekeeping operations and the opportunity costs of lost investment and trade.

The United States and the international community's experience with failed states in other regions of the world (including Colombia, which is sometimes referred to as a failing state) clearly shows the destabilizing influence that a failed or failing state can have on other countries in the region. The pervasive corruption in the failed state often serves to corrupt government officials in neighboring states, resulting in the erosion of democratic institutions and of the neighboring countries' political will to combat transnational threats. The safe haven provided by the failed state allows international criminal organizations a place to conduct their illegal activities without government interference. This freedom of action in turn undermines the legitimacy of the government in the ungoverned areas and leads to greater regional instability. If allowed to continue unchecked, this regional instability will compromise U.S. ability to count on its regional allies in the fight against international crime. It will also undermine the consolidation of democracy, which is ongoing in many countries in the region and is the best hope for long-term peace, stability, and economic prosperity.

Nation-Building Requirements for Haiti

Previous crises in Haiti have demonstrated which nations and multinational organizations are willing to contribute to the humanitarian assistance, peacekeeping operations, and development efforts required to stabilize Haiti. Among the nations that have proved willing to significantly contribute to these three types of efforts are the United States, Canada, and France. In addition, several multinational organizations have been instrumental in assisting Haiti; these include the United Nations, the OAS, the European Union, Caricom, the international financial institutions (IFIs), and various NGOs.

Critical to multinational humanitarian assistance efforts around the world are NGOs and international organizations (IOs), such as World Vision International and the U.N. World Food Program, which operate in many different countries and have developed great expertise and procedures for providing food, medical care, and other humanitarian services. Governmental organizations, such as the U.S. Agency for International Development (USAID), often use the NGOs and their established procedures to distribute the humanitarian relief supplies provided by the government. This is very effective because the NGOs and IOs already have people on the ground providing humanitarian assistance with their organizations' own relief supplies.

The U.N. effort in Haiti will require comprehensive humanitarian assistance, peacekeeping operations, and a development plan that will synchronize its efforts with those of the donor nations, other multinational organizations, and NGOs. The complexity of this operation is such that the U.N. management team will have to be established and remain in Haiti for the duration. [Former] U.N. secretary-general Kofi Annan warned that the efforts to help rebuild Haiti's police, judiciary, and other institutions will take 10 years or more. The secretary-general planned to appoint a special representative for Haiti [Juan Gabriel Valdés of Chile]. The U.N. Security Council authorized both the U.S.–led 3,600-person Multinational Interim Force–Haiti, which provided security and stability for three months until June 1 [2004], when the first 80 troops of the Brazil-led U.N. Peacekeeping Operations Force arrived. The U.N. force, with a six-month mandate, includes troops from Brazil, Argentina, Canada, Chile, France, Nepal, Rwanda, and other nations. The projected 8,000-person U.N. force will consist of 6,700 troops and 1,622 civilian police. The follow-on U.N. operation should resemble the structure of the former U.N. Mission in Haiti, which operated there from 1994 to 2001, but the new mission must remain long enough to achieve developmental success. The OAS and Caricom should also use the special representative structure to closely monitor operations in Haiti, including their own organizational contributions, and to keep the organizations' leadership and member nations informed as to progress in Haiti.

The U.S. effort in Haiti will likewise require a comprehensive plan to synchronize the efforts of the various departments of the U.S. government. In 1997, under the Clinton administration, Presidential Decision Directive 56 established the structure for this comprehensive interagency planning and mandated that for complex contingency operations (such as

Haiti), a Political-Military Implementation Plan would be developed as an integrated planning tool. Another structure that assisted Haiti during 1995 to 1997 was the U.S. Military Support Group, which remained in Haiti to provide engineering, civil affairs, and medical assistance efforts once the initial U.S. military forces had been withdrawn. Reestablishing this structure, with a similar role for these military capabilities, would be a valuable part of the overall U.S. assistance effort. The United States should also appoint a special representative or presidential envoy for Haiti to ensure that the country receives high-level attention and adequate resources. This person would also keep the U.S. government well informed about the progress of this complex operation.

Avoiding Previous Failures

We know from experience that a short-term humanitarian assistance and peacekeeping operation in Haiti will not be sufficient to avoid a similar crisis within the next decade. The only way to reestablish democracy in Haiti and overcome its problems is to invest heavily in a multinational, long-term development effort that will result in political stability, economic growth, and social progress. This will require sustained political will and adequate resources provided by numerous concerned nations, multinational organizations, and NGOs. Only through a long-term committed partnership can we hope to provide Haiti the opportunity to enjoy the benefits of a truly democratic society. The quick-exit strategies of the past and the short time lines for development assistance must be replaced by a new mind-set of long-term development assistance, without fixed time lines, if we are to avoid a repeat of previous crises.

| *"The dirty little secret of nation building is that no one knows how to do it."*

Nation-Building Is Not a Hope for Failed States

James L. Payne

James L. Payne argues in this viewpoint that nation-building is a mirage, a product of misinterpreted history. He does not believe any nation can claim an expertise in nation-building, and some of the most quoted famous examples were not successful in terms defined by other political writers, such as the British and American intervention in Italy following World War II. Payne claims that nation-building often frustrates and inhibits democracy. James L. Payne is a political scientist whose latest book is A History of Force: Exploring the Worldwide Movement Against Habits of Coercion, Bloodshed, and Mayhem.

As you read, consider the following questions:

1. According to Payne, are long nation-building occupations the most effective?

2. Why did Lieutenant Colonel John T. Fischel feel that the strategy for U.S. forces occupying Panama in 1989 was meaningless, according to the viewpoint author?

James L. Payne, "Does Nation Building Work?" *The Independent Review*, vol. 10, no. 4, spring 2006, pp. 599-610. www.independent.org. Copyright © 2006. Reproduced by permission of The Independent Institute, 100 Swan Way, Oakland, CA 94021-1428.

3. Successful establishment of democracy during military occupation and nation-building is usually the result of what, according to Payne?

In plunging into war, hope generally triumphs over experience. The past—the quiet statistical tabulation of what happened when such plunges were taken before—tends to be ignored in the heat of angry oratory and the thump of military boots. At the outset, it is easy to believe that force will be successful in upholding virtue and that history has no relevance.

Lately, this confidence in the force of arms has centered on nation building—that is, on invading and occupying a land afflicted by dictatorship or civil war and turning it into a democracy. This objective has been a major theme of the U.S. government's actions in Iraq [beginning in 2003] and Afghanistan [beginning in 2001] but the policy is not likely to be limited to those countries. The U.S. government now enjoys a military preeminence in the world, and the temptation to deploy its armed forces to repair or transform other regimes is likely to prove attractive again in the future.

Nation-Building by Force

Moreover, the idea of invading countries to "fix" them has recently gained considerable support in the academic and foreign-policy community. Among the first to advocate the assertive use of U.S. military forces around the world were [foreign policy analysts] William Kristol and Robert Kagan. In a 1996 article in *Foreign Affairs*, they urged the United States to adapt a posture of "benevolent global hegemony." This means "actively promoting American principles of governance abroad—democracy, free markets, respect for liberty." To John Quincy Adams's advice that America should not go "abroad in search of monsters to destroy," they mockingly replied, "But why not?" In their endorsement for foreign-policy activism, Kagan and Kristol have been joined by a number of policy wonks, journalists, and academics, a group that has come to be known as "neoconservatives."

In their enthusiasm for nation building by force of arms, neither the theorists nor the practitioners have examined the historical experience with this kind of policy. They are aware that a historical record exists, but they do not take it seriously. In a [March 6, 2003] speech two weeks before the invasion of Iraq, President George W. Bush pointed to other interventions that had been successful:

> America has made and kept this kind of commitment before—in the peace that followed a world war. After defeating enemies, we did not leave behind occupying armies, we left constitutions and parliaments. We established an atmosphere of safety, in which responsible, reform-minded local leaders could build lasting institutions of freedom. In societies that once bred fascism and militarism, liberty found a permanent home. There was a time when many said that the cultures of Japan and Germany were incapable of sustaining democratic values. Well, they were wrong. . . .

Democracy Evolves on Its Own

In assessing the effectiveness of nation-building efforts, we need to be careful not to confuse conjunction with cause. That some military interventions have been *followed by* democracy does not mean that the interventions *caused* the democracy. [T]here is a worldwide movement against the use of force, and this trend promotes democratic development. Rulers are becoming less disposed to use violence to repress oppositions, and government critics are less inclined to resort to armed force against rulers. The result of this broad, historical trend is that countries are becoming democracies on their own, without any outside help. After all, most of the democracies in the world have come about in this way, by internal evolution. No one invaded Britain or Holland or Finland or Costa Rica to turn them into democracies, and the same holds for many other countries. This trend has to be kept in mind in evaluating the "success" of a nation-building effort.

For example, we might be tempted to praise the British occupation of Malaysia for "bringing" democracy to that country. In the same period, however, Thailand, which had not been occupied, also joined the camp of democratic nations. In fact, in the Freedom House [organization supporting global democracy, mainly funded by the U.S. government] survey of political rights and civil liberties, Thailand ranks ahead of Malaysia. It is quite possible, then, that Malaysia would have become as democratic as it is today without British intervention.

South Korea presents an interesting lesson in the effectiveness of democratic tutelage. Beginning in 1945, when the U.S. troops landed after World War II, the United States was heavily involved in guiding political decisions in South Korea. This political involvement essentially ceased after 1961, and the South Koreans were allowed to go their own way politically. That way proved to be a military dictatorship under General Park Chung-Hee, which lasted until his murder by other officials in 1979. Thereafter followed two coups, a violent uprising in Kwangju [southern South Korean city], and many bloody street demonstrations. By 1985, however, the suppression of civil liberties had been greatly relaxed, and competitive elections were held. Since that time, South Korea can be called a democracy (albeit a noisy one with plenty of corruption). So here is a case in which sixteen years of tutelage under the Americans brought failure with regard to the establishment of democracy, but the country evolved to democracy on its own twenty-five years after U.S. involvement in local politics ceased.

Assessing Nation-Building

In deciding whether nation-building efforts work, therefore, it is not enough to show that some occupations are followed by democracy. The key question is: Does democracy emerge more frequently in the occupied countries than in nations evolving on their own? Because of the difficulty of defining a proper control group, this question cannot be given a definitive answer. It is clear, however, that once autonomous democratic development is taken into account, the apparent nation-building successes, meager as they are to begin with, are themselves probably only spurious proof of the nation builders' claims.

For example, at first glance, it might seem that the U.S. intervention in the Dominican Republic in 1965 brought democracy to that country. But consider the larger trend in Latin America. Almost all the countries in this region were not democracies at the start of the twentieth century, but almost all have evolved to a democratic politics now. It is quite possible, then, that the Dominican Republic would have become a democracy on its own. Indeed, some observers believe that this change was already under way in 1965. Moreover, they believe the U.S. intervention aborted a middle-class democratic revolution that was on the verge of succeeding (U.S. officials feared—on perhaps flimsy evidence—that it would be taken over by [Cuban leader Fidel] Castro Communists). Thus, one can with justice say that the United States did not "bring" democracy to the Dominican Republic in 1965. It was already coming, and the U.S. action merely delayed its arrival by a year or two.

Does Anyone Know How to Do This?

Another way to assess the effectiveness of nation building is to examine the time dimension. If nation building were an effective therapy, then it should follow that the longer it is applied, the more certain its success will be. To use the medical analogy, the nation-building "doctors" will be more likely to cure the patient if they can apply their vital therapy over a longer period of time. The idea that longer military occupations are more effective in creating democracy is widely believed. Among those who take this position is Richard Haass, the president of the Council on Foreign Relations and formerly

Nation-building Military Occupations by the United States and Great Britain, 1850–2000

U.S. Occupations

Austria 1945–1955 success

Cuba 1898–1902 failure

Cuba 1906–1909 failure

Cuba 1917–1922 failure

Dominican Republic 1911–1924 failure

Dominican Republic 1965–1967 success

Grenada 1983–1985 success

Haiti 1915–1934 failure

Haiti 1994–1996 failure

Honduras 1924 failure

Italy 1943–1945 success

Japan 1945–1952 success

Lebanon 1958 failure

Lebanon 1982–1984 failure

Mexico 1914–1917 failure

Nicaragua 1909–1910 failure

Nicaragua 1912–1925 failure

Nicaragua 1926–1933 failure

Panama 1903–1933 failure

Panama 1989–1995 success

Philippines 1898–1946 success

Somalia 1992–1994 failure

South Korea 1945–1961 failure

West Germany 1945–1952 success

British Occupations

Botswana 1886–1966 success

Brunei 1888–1984 failure

Burma (Myanmar) 1885–1948 failure

Cyprus 1914–1960 failure

Egypt 1882–1922 failure

Fiji 1874–1970 success

Ghana 1886–1957 failure

Iraq 1917–1932 failure

Iraq 1941–1947 failure

Jordan 1921–1956 failure

Kenya 1894–1963 failure

Lesotho 1884–1966 failure

Malawi (Nyasaland) 1891–1964 failure

Malaysia 1909–1957 success

Maldives 1887–1976 success

Nigeria 1861–1960 failure

Palestine 1917–1948 failure

Sierra Leone 1885–1961 failure

Solomon Islands 1893–1978 success

South Yemen (Aden) 1934–1967 failure

Sudan 1899–1956 failure

Swaziland 1903–1968 failure

Tanzania 1920–1963 failure

Tonga 1900–1970 success

Uganda 1894–1962 failure

Zambia (N. Rhodesia) 1891–1964 failure

Zimbabwe (S. Rhodesia) 1888–1980 failure

TAKEN FROM: James L. Payne, "Deconstructing Nation-Building," *American Conservative* Magazine, October 24, 2005. www.amconmag .com.

the director of policy planning for the [U.S.] State Department during the invasion of Iraq. Haass asserts that "[i]t is one thing to oust a regime, quite another to put something better in its place. Prolonged occupation of the sort the United States carried out in Japan and West Germany after World War II is the only surefire way to build democratic institutions and instill democratic culture."

Are "prolonged" occupations really more effective? The facts contradict this claim. The United States has been involved in many occupations much longer than the seven years in West Germany, but it has failed in most cases. The United States occupied and administered Haiti from 1915 to 1934. Those nineteen years of control proved not to be a "surefire" route to democracy, but merely an interlude in a violent and chaotic politics that continues to this day. Other cases of long U.S. interventions that failed to establish democracy include Nicaragua (1912), thirteen years; Nicaragua (1926), seven years; the Dominican Republic (1911), thirteen years; and Panama (1903), thirty years.

The British experience confirms the point. Numerous former British colonies had sixty, seventy, and more years of occupation and administration, yet failed to sustain democracy after the British left. For example, Zimbabwe, much in the news today because of dictator Robert Mugabe's extreme actions, experienced ninety-two years of British administration. Other long-occupied countries that failed to sustain democracy after the British left include Nigeria (ninety-nine years), Sierra Leone (seventy-six years), Ghana (seventy-one years), and Burma (sixty-three years).

That long occupations so often fail to establish stable democracies indicates that something is seriously wrong with the medical model of nation building. The "doctors" apparently do not have an effective therapy. Indeed, a close look reveals that they have no therapy at all. The dirty little secret of nation building is that *no one knows how to do it.* Huge amounts of government and foundation money have been poured into this question, and, in response to the dollars, the scholars and bureaucrats have produced only reams of verbose commentary. Even after all these efforts, no concrete, usable body of knowledge exists, no methodology of how "to build democratic institutions and instill democratic culture," as Haass puts it.

There are no experts on nation building. The people who end up doing the so-called nation building are simply ordinary government employees who wind up at the scene of the military occupation. Many times they are military officers with no background in politics, sociology, or social psychology (not that it would help them, in any case). For the most part, these government employees see their mission as that of trying to get themselves and the U.S. forces out of the country without too much egg on their faces. They have no clearer idea of how to "instill democratic culture" than does the proverbial man on the street.

Pursuing an Undefined Goal

A look at some specific examples of nation building illustrates the intellectual vacuum. The U.S. invasion of Panama in 1989 is credited as a nation-building success. Was this positive outcome the result of the expert application of political science? One of the nation builders, [U.S.] Lieutenant Colonel John T. Fishel, has written a book on the Panama experience that paints quite a different picture. Fishel was chief of policy and strategy for U.S. forces in Panama, and his job was to figure out how to implement the mission statement. The orders looked simple on paper: "Conduct nation building operations to ensure democracy." Fishel quickly discovered, however, that the instruction was meaningless because democracy was an "undefined goal." It seemed to him that it was not the job of military officers to figure out how to implement this undefined objective, but, as he observes with a touch of irritation, "there are no U.S. civilian strategists clearly articulating strategies to achieve democracy." Worse, "[t]he fact that there was no clear definition of the conditions that constitute democracy meant that the [U.S.] Military Support Group and the other U.S. government agencies that were attempting to assist the [President Guillermo] Endara government [in power 1990–1994] had only the vaguest concept of what actions and programs would lead the country toward democracy." In practice, the goal of "ensuring democracy" boiled down to installing Guillermo Endara, the winner of a previous election, as president, supporting him as he became increasingly highhanded and unpopular, and then stepping away after his opponent was elected in 1994. Not exactly rocket science. . . .

The interventions in Afghanistan [2001] and Iraq [2003] further illustrate how haphazard and unfocused nation building is in practice. Neither of these efforts has followed any plan, design, or theory for establishing a democracy. In invading Afghanistan, the Bush administration gave little thought to political arrangements that might follow military victory over the Taliban. Less than three weeks before the attack, President Bush asked national-security advisor Condoleezza Rice, "Who will run the country?" It was a moment of panic for her because she had not given the issue any thought.

[In 2003] with the invasion of Iraq, the administration had apparently gained nothing in nation-building expertise. Although the military campaign was a success, the occupation and its administration have been characterized by naïveté and improvisation. In the early stages of the invasion, the U.S. government had neither a policy to check looting nor the forces to do so—policymakers had apparently forgotten the lesson of Panama—and the result was a ravaging of local infrastructure, the rapid formation of gangs of thugs and paramilitary fighters, and a loss of local support for the U.S. effort. The civilian administration was first put in the hands of retired [U.S] Lieutenant General Jay Garner, who was two weeks late getting to Baghdad and who naively expected to find a functioning government in the country. After one month, the hapless Garner was fired, and Paul Bremer was appointed his replacement as chief administrator. Two months after the invasion, Lieutenant General William Wallace, the [U.S. Army] Fifth Corps commander, described the nation-building "technique" that U.S. officials were applying in Iraq: "We're making this up here as we go along."

Evolution Trumps Nation-Building

Trying to establish democracy through military occupation is not a coherent, defensible policy. There is no theory on which it is based; it has no proven technique or methodology; and no experts know how to do it. The record shows that it usually fails, and even when it appears to succeed, the positive result owes more to historical evolution and local political culture than to anything the nation builders might have done.

> "Unless adequate attention is given to health, nation-building efforts cannot be successful."

Public Health Care Is Necessary for Successful Nation-Building

Seth G. Jones et al.

In this viewpoint, Seth G. Jones and his coauthors argue that establishing a public health infrastructure, even in the midst of chaotic nation-building and military occupation events, is critical to regenerating decaying nations. Although other factors, such as security, are important influences on nation-building, the authors argue that health care is understudied and may be a remedy for failing reconstruction efforts when properly applied. Seth G. Jones is a nation-building policy analyst at the RAND Corporation.

As you read, consider the following questions:

1. According to the authors, inadequate health care can have a negative effect on security in nation-building situations. What are the negative effects?

Seth G. Jones et al., *Securing Health Lessons from Nation-Building Missions*, RAND Center for Domestic and International Health Security, 2006. Copyright © 2006 RAND Corporation. All rights reserved. Reproduced by permission.

2. Past nation-building experiences show one party should be the lead in health care reconstruction of nation-states. Who should that lead be, according to the authors?

3. The ultimate object of rebuilding a health care delivery system should be to reach what, according to the viewpoint authors?

Unless adequate attention is given to health, nation-building efforts cannot be successful. Indeed, health can have an important independent impact on nation-building and overall development. Several of the cases show that security is significantly impacted by the role health plays in helping to win "hearts and minds," an objective whose importance is illustrated by cases such as Iraq and Somalia. In both of these cases, the inability to win hearts and minds contributed to insurgency, warlordism, and an unstable security environment. Counterinsurgency experts have long argued that winning hearts and minds is a key—if not *the* key—component in establishing peace. Health can play an important role in the effort by, for example, offering tangible health programs to the local population and meeting basic health needs, such as improving sanitation and nutrition conditions. Such programs should be designed to gain support for the host country, rather than for the United States or other outside actors; the local government should be the entity winning the hearts and minds of the population. In the early stages of nation-building operations, the absence of a local government may make it difficult to win hearts and minds. This was the case during the operations in Germany, Somalia, Kosovo, and Iraq. Over time, however, political authority invariably shifts to local control. When it does, programs must be designed to gain support for the local government.

Poor Health Care Helps Insurgents

Health can have an important negative effect on security, as well. In [the U.S. occupation, begun in 2003, of] Iraq, for example, there is some evidence that poor health conditions—especially poor sanitation conditions—contributed to anti-Americanism and support for the insurgency. Most early reconstruction efforts in the Iraqi health sector went into activities that were not immediately visible to Iraqis, such as establishing a surveillance system and creating a statistical database of hospitals and clinics.

Maximizing the effectiveness of health as an independent variable means paying close attention to the sequence of health steps. Nation-building programs will generally follow three broad, sequenced phases: immediate post-conflict, reconstruction, and consolidation. During the immediate post-conflict phase, at least three types of emergency health situations should take priority. Failure to address them well or quickly can complicate reconstruction in other areas and lead to animosity among the local population, whereas success can help win hearts and minds. First, the clinical consequences arising after the use of weapons of mass destruction must be quickly and adequately addressed. In [WWII] Japan [after the atom bomb explosions at Hiroshima and Nagasaki], this was not done; the treatment of survivors was left largely to the Japanese themselves. Allied doctors eventually brought in penicillin and plasma, but the slow and inadequate treatment of victims contributed to high casualty rates. Second, the outbreak—or potential outbreak—of communicable diseases needs to be met quickly to prevent spreading. Third, basic public health needs, such as food and sanitation, should be met as quickly as possible. Famine has been a particular concern. After Somali President Siad Barre was deposed in 1991, an estimated 300,000 people died of starvation over the next two years. The United Nations and United States provided immediate humanitarian assistance and saved an estimated additional 300,000 Somalis from famine.

The Web Around the Health Sector

Health conditions are deeply impacted by other key sectors, including security, basic infrastructure (such as power and transportation), education, governance, and economic stabilization. [Economist] Amartya Sen argues that the linkages between these sectors are empirical and causal:

> [T]here is strong evidence that economic and political freedoms help to reinforce one another. . . . Similarly, social opportunities of education and health care, which may require public action, complement individual opportunities of economic and political participation and also help to foster our own initiatives in overcoming our respective deprivations.

The health sector is particularly sensitive to security in at least two ways: through direct effects, such as the inability of patients to visit doctors; and through indirect effects, such as the inability of health care facilities to function properly. A lack of security can impede progress in the reconstruction of water plants and hospitals, slow immunization campaigns, restrict delivery of needed supplies to health care facilities, and affect the labor force if health care providers are intimidated or threatened with kidnapping. Patients can also be deterred from seeking health care because of security concerns. Situations such as this (Iraq, for example), where there is a pervasive lack of security, cannot be fixed by ad hoc measures, such as providing security guards to hospitals and guarding water plants and pipes.

The success of the health sector is also tightly linked with progress in other sectors, such as basic infrastructure. In Iraq, for instance, hospitals and clinics operated at partial capacity and had to use power generators provided by international organizations. In general, a lack of clean water, sanitation, or power increases the likelihood of acute disease outbreaks or widespread epidemics, and makes it difficult to build a functioning health system. International organizations may spend time and resources refurbishing hospitals and clinics, training staff, and providing equipment. But unreliable power nullifies much of this effort. The success of the health care system is also linked to reconstruction of the financial, judicial, and education systems. For example, if financial systems are not working, it is difficult to acquire supplies and capital equipment, and equally challenging to develop health-financing mechanisms.

Planning Health Care Building

The coordination of health efforts is a key challenge during reconstruction. Indeed, the World Bank argues that past nation-building efforts have suffered from "a lack of an overarching nationally-driven plan to which all donors agree, resulting in fragmentation, gaps or duplication in aid-financed programs." Poor coordination can weaken fragile health systems by scattering assistance to an assortment of health projects and failing to sufficiently tackle key priorities.

In some ways, coordination and planning were easier in the post–World War II cases of Germany and Japan because there were fewer actors, which made it easier for government officials to coordinate policies and communicate among health personnel. The number of actors involved in health reconstruction has exponentially increased since the end of the Cold War. The greater the number of actors, the more difficult the coordination. Two steps can help improve mission coordination: encouraging and rationalizing a lead-state or lead-organization system for health, and learning from and replicating successful on-the-ground organizational innovations.

Lead Actors and Lessons Learned

First, the need to overcome coordination and collaboration problems makes it important to establish institutional arrangements that increase efficiency in rebuilding health. There are a variety of options: donor coordination units within a host state's Ministry of Health, a lead national actor, lead regional or local actors, regular collective Ministry of Health consultations with donors, and sector-wide approaches. A lead actor approach is usually the most effective coordinating strategy for planning and funding, especially when the host government is barely functional. In the health sector, experience suggests that the lead actor(s) should be an international organization rather than a state. It can be difficult to agree on a lead actor, since donor states, international institutions, and NGOs [nongovernmental organizations] generally have different priorities, interests, and strategies. But a lead actor is critical to ensure efficiency and effectiveness. This can include coordinating and overseeing the undertaking of joint assessments, preparing shared strategies, coordinating political engagement, establishing joint offices, and introducing simplified arrangements, such as common reporting and financial requirements. In theory, the lead actor can be a donor state, international organization, or NGO. In practice, however, only states and international organizations have the resources and legitimacy necessary to be lead actors. Two elements crucial to the task of establishing a lead actor are buy-in from the host government and support from key donors, international organizations, and NGOs.

Second, there is a strong need to consolidate lessons learned and best practices in coordinating activities. NGOs and other organizations have worked out effective ad hoc organizational arrangements at national and local levels to improve coordination. One important aspect should be to coordinate with international institutions or NGOs that were involved in health and health-related efforts before and during the conflict. Their experience provides an invaluable understanding of the health care system, the health status of the population, and the major health challenges within a country. Since reliable statistical information on health conditions is

Slipping Down the Development Ladder

Since 1978, by the United Nations' reckoning, the number of countries that are 'least developed' has shot up from 28 to 48. This means that one country per year has slipped down the development ranking during the last two 'development decades'. The assets of the three richest people in the world are more than the GNP [gross national product] of the 48 least developed countries, and the three richest officers of Gates' Microsoft have more assets (upwards $140 billion) than the combined GNP of the 43 least developed countries. Meanwhile, health care eludes the poor who constitute 50 percent of the population of the least developed 46 poorest countries. About two billion people in the world live on less than a (US) dollar a day, and more than 800 million people have total lack of access to any form of basic health care. Nearly three billion do not have access to safe drinking water and appropriate sanitation.

Rajashri Dasgupta, "Patients, Private Charity and Public Health," Himāl South Asian *magazine, August 2000. www.himalmag.com.*

often unavailable during the initial post-conflict phase, prior knowledge is crucial. Bilateral donors, international institutions, and NGOs should utilize actors with in-country experience to assist in coordination and planning.

Creating a Long-Term Health System

Health sector reform must encourage long-term sustainability. Indeed, the ultimate objective of health reconstruction should be to reach a "tipping point": the point at which the local government begins to assume substantial responsibility for managing the health sector. This point will be different in every nation-building case, and will likely take longer to reach in less-developed states. It took Germany approximately two and a half years to reach [in 1947] the tipping point; however, U.S. advisors continued to observe, inspect, advise, and report on health activities. Haiti never reached the tipping point. The United States largely withdrew [military nation-building operations] after three years [in 2001], and the Haitian government never developed the capacity to implement health programs and to administratively operate them.

The training of indigenous personnel is critical to sustainability. Without it, the programs neither reflect favorably on the host government nor remain effective once outside forces and personnel have departed. Another critical aspect is assessment of the national and private health institutions' capacity to engage in needs assessment and implementation. Capacity has important implications for recovery and planning. From an operational perspective, it makes sense to distinguish between two types of post-conflict situations: strong national capacities and weak national capacities. These distinctions should not be regarded as absolute, but as two ends of a continuum. Most countries are located between these extremes.

In countries with strong national health capacities, such as Germany after World War II, health progress may be more rapid. Since national contributions and ownership are likely to be high, planning can be oriented beyond the short-term (0 to 18 months) to include the medium-term (18 to 36 months) recovery and development needs. In countries with weak health capacities, national and private health institutions usually lack the capacity to make substantial contributions to the needs assessment and implementation. In Somalia, warlords did not support relief efforts and attacked, looted, or extorted payments from relief convoys. In Afghanistan, tribes and local strongmen, rather than the central government, have historically controlled most of the country, making it difficult to create a self-sufficient and sustainable health system. The variation in initial nation-building conditions places a premium on correct determination of governance institution effectiveness and the nature of the conflict. Much like Afghanistan, states with a weak national capacity can face a series of challenges after major conflict:

- Severely deteriorating health conditions, especially if civilians and civilian structures were targets of violence

- Institutional collapse

- Social cleavages between groups manipulated by the parties to the conflict

- Lack of accountability mechanisms because there is no legitimate government

Development and Health Care Recovery

The curves of decline and recovery are likely to be different for these cases, especially when there has been a long-term degradation of health. Challenges are deeper, and progress should be expected to be slower before reaching a tipping point. The health infrastructure, administrative capacity, and physical infrastructure may have ceased to exist—or may never have existed at all. Such situations require a reconstruction effort strongly shaped by the goal of development. In Afghanistan, the international community geared up for a standard post-conflict reconstruction effort instead of acknowledging that what it largely faced was a development challenge.

If development is the goal, an important question arises: Will health recovery plans perpetuate a tradition of national dependence on the external design, delivery, and financing of health care that will jeopardize sustainability? Unfortunately, the main health challenges in countries with weak national capacities are not amenable to quick fixes. The population must become stronger and healthier through improved nutrition and access to clean water and sanitation. A new generation of health care professionals has to be recruited, trained, and motivated to work in rural areas. Some long-standing habits and attitudes, particularly related to marriage, family, and the status of women, must change. And the country needs years of stability and security for these changes to occur and take hold.

Time Is Critical

Short-term medical care is valuable, but to change a state's health care system requires time and sustained effort. In Haiti and Somalia, for example, outside powers wanted to withdraw as fast as possible. The search for a fixed exit strategy is illusory, if this means a certain date in the near future when full control of health care facilities can be handed back to local authorities. Exit requires a functioning health care system that has at least reached the tipping point.

Duration is a critical variable and cuts across all aspects of reconstruction. Based on the cases we examined, no effort to rebuild health after major combat has been successful in less than five years. The cases of postwar Germany and Japan underestimate the time needed to rebuild health because both countries were fairly developed in 1945. Nation-building efforts in developing countries, such as Somalia and Afghanistan in this study, would have to continue for much longer than five years to be successful. With little health infrastructure to begin with, such countries require the time needed to achieve local buy-in, build hospitals and clinics, conduct immunization programs, train health personnel, and improve sanitation and nutrition conditions.

An interesting point about duration is that while staying for a long time does not always guarantee success, leaving early usually assures failure. U.S.–led efforts to rebuild Somalia and Haiti were short-lived. The bulk of health assistance lasted for only three years, and continuing political instability in Haiti led the international community to withhold all aid by 2000. The cost of early departures is clear: It is difficult to ensure success in rebuilding health. . . .

Judging Success

What are the policy implications of rebuilding health for international institutions, NGOs, and donor states? . . . Afghanistan and Iraq, have reinforced well-worn lessons. Of the many lessons about health and nation-building that the international community learned during the 1990s, few have been applied in Afghanistan or Iraq.

Applying these lessons will not ipso facto guarantee success. But, on the basis of our findings, we believe it will vastly improve the chances of success, as measured by improvements in sanitation conditions, infectious disease rates, mortality and morbidity rates, and nutrition conditions. Our findings also support the use of these metrics as criteria by which to judge success. Given the likelihood of future nation-building missions, it may be worthwhile for interdisciplinary experts to define the possible dimensions of "success." While each nation-building mission will, of course, differ somewhat in overall objectives and data availability, it is nonetheless critical to develop a framework for monitoring and measuring inputs and outputs.

> "The strength of the West in relation to the East has never been in its impositions and colonialisms."

Nation-Building Fuels Civil Destruction

Pierre Tristam

Pierre Tristam argues in this viewpoint that the U.S. nation-building in Iraq mimics circumstances involving the United States in Southeast Asia over thirty years ago. In both instances, he believes the United States has exaggerated its nation-building efforts to cover up the destruction it wages against the societies it is involved with. Tristam predicts, based on his historical reading, the United States will blame the Arabs for our own failures in Iraq and elsewhere. Pierre Tristam is an editorial writer and columnist at the Daytona Beach News Journal, *and editor of* Candide's Notebooks.

As you read, consider the following questions:

1. When U.S. neoconservatives celebrated the invasion of Iraq as a turning point in Middle East democracy, what did they ignore, according to Tristam?

Pierre Tristam, "Iraq's Cambodian Jungle: How American 'Nation-Building' Fueled Civil War," *Candide's Notebooks*, February 24, 2006. www.pierretristam.com. Reproduced by permission.

2. According to Tristam, how has the United States used the story of Muslim on Muslim violence in Iraq?

3. Does the author believe that another genocide could happen in Iraq despite U.S. nation-building efforts?

The standard line about Iraq [as of February 2006] is that the country is *on the verge of civil war.* That "simmering hatreds" are boiling to the surface. That "sectarianism" is to blame. All those regurgitated clichés of the Orientalist [studies of Near and Far East cultures by Western scholars] canon may well be true. But what convenient detractions from a three-year-old certainty rendered by the American invasion. What ideal way to shift the blame, indemnify the invader, and make this [March 2006] third anniversary of Iraq's "liberation," approaching at the speed of a panicked Bradley Fighting Vehicle [U.S. Army tank], look like a job gone awry only because Iraqis couldn't get along. Sure, the destruction of a revered Shiite mosque in Samarra, allegedly by Sunni militants, was not going to get a kinder reception than the destruction of the 16th Century Babri mosque in Ayodhya, in India, by Hindus, in December 1992. That barbaric eruption led to riots across India and Pakistan that left more than 1,000 people dead and renewed fears of a sectarian breakdown on the subcontinent, possibly even another reason for India and Pakistan to go at it a fourth time in six decades. The fears were exaggerated. The discovery that religion is south Asia's radioactive variant was not. It's that very variant the neo-cons [neoconservatives] ignored when they celebrated the invasion of Iraq as a turning point in Mideastern destiny.

Military Force Is Not Nation-Building

It has been a turning point, with the wrong assumptions at gunpoint. The problem wasn't Iraq's WMDs [weapons of mass destruction] or Iran's nukes. It's the region's religious warheads. There's no easier way to arm them than with Western-fueled resentment, no quicker way to set them off than with the permanent reminder of an alien army of *provocateurs*, the same Anglo provocateurs whose boots not so long ago, in every grandfather's memory, flattened the culture with colonialism and called it progress. Conversely, there are more credible, more Wilsonian ways to diffuse the warheads, beginning with Woodrow Wilson's aversion to assuming mandates and protectorates over regions better left to sort out their issues on their own, but with available help when requested.

That's the approach Francis Fukuyama, the ex-neocon, is now advocating in his belated berating of the neocon catastrophe in Iraq: "[T]he United States does not get to decide when and where democracy comes about. By definition, outsiders can't 'impose' democracy on a country that doesn't want it; demand for democracy and reform must be domestic. Democracy promotion is therefore a long-term and opportunistic process that has to await the gradual ripening of political and economic conditions to be effective." In other words, the so-called "liberal" approach advocated all along by those who don't see bombs as quite compatible with democratic nation-building.

The strength of the West in relation to the East has never been in its impositions and colonialisms. That's when it's been at its weakest, at its most repugnant, morally and politically. Western strength has been derived, paradoxically, from restraint: by valuing example above force, persuasion above imposition. (World War I and II were not battles between East and West but primarily *within* the West.) That strength, at the moment, has been made null and void by the American occupation of Iraq—by Abu Ghraib [torture of Iraqis by U.S. personnel at this Iraqi prison], by Guantanamo [Bay, Cuba, where the United States holds enemy combatants deemed terrorists], by the parody of democracy in Afghanistan and the emerging tragedy of democracy in Iraq, Iran and Palestine, where extremism is not only ascendant, but triumphant and virtually unrivaled.

Muslim Nation-Building

How did poverty-stricken Cambodia and its [Cham] Muslim population of 700,000 find itself enmeshed in the international war on terrorism? Some scholars point back to the Khmer Rouge years, which left the devastated country reliant on outside aid, Islamic and otherwise. . . .

Shortly after the Khmer Rouge was deposed in 1979, some Cham began to make connections with the outside Islamic community. The largest influx of aid began during the United Nations' nation-building efforts in 1992 and 1993. A number of those peacekeepers and aid workers were from Muslim countries, and after Cambodia held its first elections in 1993, money from Saudi Arabia, Kuwait, the United Arab Emirates, and Malaysia began flowing into Cham communities to sponsor pilgrimages to Mecca, build mosques and Islamic schools, and provide other religious and social services. . . .

Today, as the Cham struggle to rebuild their communities, fundamentalists and jihadists may have found a ripe target: an impoverished minority population in need of aid and a reconnection to Islam.

Noy Thrupkaew, "Follow the (Saudi) Money,"
The American Prospect *online, August 1, 2004. www.prospect.org.*

Replacing One Tyranny with Another

Iraq is not "on the verge" of civil war. It has been at war the moment Americans replaced one tyranny with a pluralism of tyrannies three years ago. Iran blamed the explosion in Samarra on Israel and the United States. Israel, of course, has nothing whatsoever to do with Iraq. But American responsibility for Samarra is as evident as American responsibility for the looting and chaos that followed the early days of the occupation—and of course the chaos and low-grade civil war that hasn't stopped since. The powder keg was always there. It was to be a sign of American wiles and strategy—of foresight or ignorance—either to diffuse the keg or light the match. With Bush at the helm, the American occupation had no choice but to suck fire. That fuse is what the Anglo-American occupation force represents in Iraq. The Orientalist narrative of Muslim-on-Muslim violence happening as if in a vacuum all its own is the expedient way for Western conservatives to translate the latest events to their convenience. It's also an opportunity. Here's the Bush administration's chance to claim that it's done all it could. Sectarian battles aren't its game (South Carolina's Republican primary [in 2000] *fatwa* [legal ruling in Islamic law] against [Senator] John McCain notwithstanding). Time to go. Time to let them sort it out. The going won't be literal, to be sure: The administration isn't oiling those permanent military bases for nothing, nor does it want to have an Arab Yalta [southern Ukrainian city where leaders of the United States, UK, and Soviet Union met at the end of WWII] tattooed on its retreating rear. No, this would be a stealth retreat from the turbulence of the Iraqi street to the safety of U.S. garrisons on the barbarians' rims, something even [former marine and U.S. congressman since 1974] John Murtha could applaud. No retreat, no surrender, but redeployment. At least for now.

Nation-Building as Civil War

But it's the Cambodian get-away scheme all over again: [U.S. president Richard] Nixon bombs Cambodia back to the Neolithic from 1970 to 1973, killing somewhere in the six figures, destabilizing the country with [Cambodian president] Lon Nol's complicity and setting the stage for the Khmer [Rouge] take-over and ensuing genocide. Nixon shrugs, acts blameless. It was a civil war, after all, and he had his own civil war on his hands, compliments of a couple of reporters from the *Washington Post* [who were breaking the Watergate scandal, leading to Nixon's resignation]. With Kissinger as his [Wizard of] Oz, Nixon spun Cambodia into just another American attempt at battling Communism in the name of freedom. The Khmers mucked it up. And by 1973, Kissinger was throwing in the towel, Nixon was facing impeachment, and the Khmers were biding their time until their final, if brief, victory in 1975 (until the Vietnamese finally ended their killing spree in 1978). A similar scenario is unfolding in Iraq. The United States has done nothing if not destabilize the country under the guise of building up democracy [since 2003]. Bombings and night raids tend not to do democracy's bidding. Insurgents have picked up strength. On both sides. A Khmer-like genocide might not be in the offing, although with [the wars in] Lebanon and the Balkans in recent memory, and with [Iraqi leader] Saddam [Hussein's] tradition of facile massacres still humidifying the Mesopotamian air with the scent of unavenged blood, you never know: a genocide may well result still, giving the region's Vietnam—Iran—an opportunity to intervene. The moment the United States invaded the way it did, and occupied the nation as boorishly as it did, the outcome couldn't have been any different than it is now. It isn't the Arabs who are repeating history. It is the United States repeating its own, a few time zones to the east. Same continent. Same errors, same Nixonian hubris.

Naturally, Arabs—those "barbaric" Sunnis and Shiites—will get all the blame. But the vilest fanatics are in the White House, comfortably enabling destruction from their "situation room." The only difference between them and the barbarians who blow up mosques is a matter of dress and language, and, of course, method. The results are the same.

> *"Violence [in East Timor] raises questions about international commitment to the tiny Asian state and highlights the difficulties in sustaining nation-building projects, no matter how small."*

UN Nation-Building May Not Last

Robert McMahon

Robert McMahon describes how the UN nation-building effort in East Timor, once viewed as one of the agency's most successful nation-building operations, deteriorated after 1999, erasing many of the gains experts thought would be long-lasting. His viewpoint describes how the UN might go about providing nation-building leadership in the future based on previous cases in other countries. Robert McMahon is the deputy editor of Council on Foreign Relations' publications.

As you read, consider the following questions:

1. How does an emerging nation like East Timor confuse UN nation-building experts, according to the viewpoint author?

2. According to UN peacekeeping chief Jean-Marie Guéhenno, what is one of the negative events that can occur due to slow nation-building?

3. What should be the mission of the new UN Peacebuilding Commission, according to the viewpoint author?

[2006] unrest in East Timor tarnishes what had been considered one of the few recent successes in UN nation-building. The United Nations shepherded the former Indonesian province to statehood after violence erupted in the aftermath of an independence referendum in 1999. But most of the 11,000-member international presence was gone by last year. The new outbreak in violence raises questions about international commitment to the tiny Asian state and highlights the difficulties in sustaining nation-building projects, no matter how small. Experts say the newly created UN Peacebuilding Commission could provide more consistency and sophistication in stabilizing post-conflict societies. But they are doubtful of long-term success without major actors' involvement.

In the aftermath of East Timor's violent separation from Indonesia in 1999, a UN administration, initially backed by Australian peacekeepers, guided the province to elections, a constitution, and formal statehood in 2002. A UN force of military observers, police, and 5,000 soldiers remained until 2003 to maintain stability. The last peacekeepers left in 2005 amid growing concerns that their departure was premature. After the government sought to dismiss nearly 600 soldiers from the army in April, violence flared and degenerated into gang warfare in the streets of the capital, Dili. The initial violence killed more than twenty people and forced more than 100,000 people—one-tenth of the country's population—to flee their homes.

Experts cite the following as causes of the instability.

Economic hardship The economy, Asia's poorest, is based mainly around coffee and oil and gas exports that do not provide ample employment for the fast-growing population. The unemployment level is about 40 percent and per capita income is about $550, according to the World Bank. Frederick Barton, a former UN deputy high commissioner for refugees and now co-director of the Post-Conflict Reconstruction Project at the Center for Strategic and International Studies, says the international system is still not sure how to handle an emerging state like East Timor. "This is an incredibly impoverished country that doesn't have any real rationale. There's no economic argument for its existence as a totally independent place, so it confuses us," Barton says. Barton and Seth Jones, a nation-building expert at the RAND Corporation, say countries like East Timor and Afghanistan are essentially at "ground zero" in terms of development and require a long period of nurturing. "You can't expect a society in three to four years to make real significant progress on basic economic and social conditions," says Jones.

Speed and Security Count

UN Peacekeeping Chief Jean-Marie Guéhenno told a recent briefing at CFR [the Council on Foreign Relations, an independent organization dedicated to analyzing foreign policy issues] that the international community has struggled to implement economic revitalization programs in post-conflict zones in a timely manner. "We see, whether it's Afghanistan after the [election of the] new parliament [in September 2005] or Haiti once the new authorities have been elected, there's a window that opens, but if in the next 24 months people do not see progress and do not have jobs [the mission] will be in trouble," Guéhenno said.

Incomplete security sector reform East Timor embarked on security sector reform in 1999 with virtually no police force.

"They were largely Indonesian and once you had this major Indonesian exodus at the end of 1999 the UN had to begin basically from scratch," says Jones. "It just takes a long time to train and then to get competent police officers." The military is reportedly beset by regional rivalries. The roughly 600 soldiers who instigated the protests come mostly from the country's west and had complained of discrimination by members from the east in the national army. An op-ed in the *Asia Times* says the fact that a few hundred disgruntled soldiers "could spark a national crisis demonstrates just how weak East Timor's Fretilin-led [political party] government still is."

Weak political institutions Domestic critics say East Timor's government has been marred by corruption and favoritism since independence was won. Local government and the judicial system are seen as weak. President Xanana Gusmao remains popular but most of the power resides in parliament, dominated by the Fretilin Party and Prime Minister Mari Alkatiri. One month into the crisis, Defense Minister Roque Rodrigues and Interior Minister Rogerio Tiago Lobato have announced their resignation. Opposition fighters are also calling for Alkatiri to step down.

Three UN Nation-Building Projects

Kosovo Seven years after the ouster of Serb forces [in 1999] the United Nations still runs the Serbian province as a virtual protectorate. But [in 2005] [former] UN Secretary-General Kofi Annan appointed Finnish diplomat Martti Ahtisaari to begin brokering final status talks between Serb and ethnic Albanian politicians. The outcome is expected to be independence for Kosovo [negotiations were ongoing as of 2006], with conditions for protecting the province's Serb minority, many of whom remain displaced. Backed by NATO [North Atlantic Treaty Organization]-led forces and international peacekeepers, the UN mission has generally retained stability

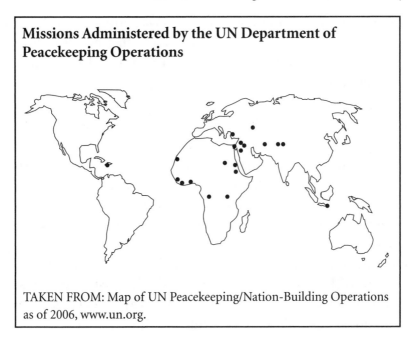

Missions Administered by the UN Department of Peacekeeping Operations

TAKEN FROM: Map of UN Peacekeeping/Nation-Building Operations as of 2006, www.un.org.

but concern about ethnic reprisals remains and the province's economy has faltered due in part to the unsettled status.

Afghanistan NATO and U.S. forces patrol the country under a UN mandate. The UN mission there guides relief, recovery, and reconstruction and provides political advice to Afghan leaders. The country has held successful presidential and parliamentary elections but its control extends to few places beyond Kabul. A resurgent Taliban, has triggered some of the fiercest fighting this spring since their expulsion in late 2001.

Liberia Nearly 15,000 UN peacekeepers support a mission charged with carrying through a three-year-old peace process that ended a devastating civil war [in 2003]. The mission also assists in police training, forming a new military and human rights activities.

The UN Peacebuilding Commission

The thirty-one-member commission was created by the UN General Assembly [in 2005] with the aim of ending the ad hoc international approach to nation-building. It seeks to bring together development, security and other actors to provide a cohesive approach to reconstruction and institution building in post-conflict zones.

Experts welcome the body but are concerned about its viability. "The peacebuilding commission is a useful concept," says Jones. "Whether it actually makes its way into substantive changes on the ground [is] too early to tell partly because for the UN to be successful, including in peacekeeping and peacebuilding operations, [it] requires cooperation among major powers that are contributing." Barton says it will be a challenge for the agency to thrive in the UN bureaucracy. The commission, he says, "will have to have an extraordinary amount of leeway, a very entrepreneurial leadership and great flexibility in funding and human resources models and real operational agility to be successful."

Nation-Building Failures

Somalia In the early 1990s, the UN Security Council authorized a U.S.–led force to establish a safe zone for assisting civilians, in reaction to a massive humanitarian crisis and a civil war. The effort spared hundreds of thousands of lives threatened by famine but was undermined by Somali militias. One attack in June 1993 killed twenty-five Pakistani peacekeepers and an Oct. 3, 1993 ambush killed eighteen U.S. soldiers and left nearly 1,000 Somalis dead. U.S. troops withdrew and the UN mission followed two years later. The country today is regarded as a failed state and fighting among various warlords continues.

Haiti The United Nations and the Organization of American States imposed sanctions on Haiti following a 1991 military coup against the democratically elected president, Jean-Bertrand Aristide. The UN Security Council authorized a U.S.–led multinational force, which entered the country in

1994, forcing out the leader of the military junta, Raoul Cedras, and restoring Aristide to the presidency. International efforts to improve the situation followed, but long-term reform of Haiti's political institutions stalled. Since the election of President Rene Preval early in 2006, there is hope that the country—the poorest in the Americas—will be able to revive efforts at economic and political reform. A UN stabilization mission of more than 8,000 is in the country [as of 2006].

Some Successes

El Salvador UN mediation helped end the civil war that ravaged the country through the 1980s and a UN mission from 1991 to 1995 helped reform and reduce the size of the armed forces, create a new police force, and reform judicial and electoral systems. The United States has been a key contributor to judicial reforms.

Eastern Slavonia Though not a full-scale nation-building project, the easternmost province of Croatia was placed under UN administration in 1996 after the war between Serbs and Croats. The UN mission oversaw the successful integration of the majority Serb area into Croatia, demilitarizing the region and ensuring the safe return of refugees to their homes as well as organizing elections.

Bosnia The former Yugoslav republic witnessed one of the UN's worst peacekeeping debacles [the 1995 massacre of Muslim civilians in Srebrenica, Bosnia, a supposed UN safe area], but since the Dayton Accords [November 1995 agreement ending fighting between Serbia, Croatia, and Bosnia] the three previously warring ethnic groups have lived in relative peace. A UN mission completed a large police restructuring project in 2002 and NATO-led forces handed over security patrols to an EU-led force in 2004.

Periodical Bibliography

The following articles have been selected to supplement the diverse views presented in this chapter.

Barbara Barungi and Karanja Mbugua	"From Peacekeeping to Peace Building: Post-Conflict Reconstruction in Africa," 2005, Association for Creative Change in Organization Renewal and Development (ACCORD), www.accord.org.
James Jay Carafano and Dana R. Dillon	"Winning the Peace: Principles for Post-Conflict Operations," The Heritage Foundation, June 13, 2005, www.heritage.org.
John D. Drolet	"Provincial Reconstruction Teams: Afghanistan vs. Iraq—Should We Have a Standard Model?" Army War College, May 1, 2006, www.carlisle.army.mil.
Ronald R. Krebs	"A School for the Nation?: How Military Service Does Not Build Nations, and How It Might," *International Security*, Spring 2004.
Rebecca Linder	"Wikis, Webs, and Networks: Creating Connections for Conflict-Prone Settings," Center for Strategic and International Studies (CSIS), October 15, 2006. www.csis.org.
Susan E. Rice	"Strengthening Weak States: A 21st Century Imperative," *Security and Peace Initiative*, August 2006, www.securitypeace.org.
Brent Scowcroft and Samuel R. Berger	"In the Wake of War: Getting Serious about Nation-Building," *The National Interest*, Fall 2005, www.nationalinterest.org.
John Shattuck	"Global Cop—Preventing Human Rights Wars in the 21st Century," *The Globalist*, February 21, 2004, www.theglobalist.com.
Workers' Daily Editors	"21st Century Security Entails Defence of Justice and Sovereignty," *Workers' Daily Internet Edition*, February 13, 2007, www.rcpbml.org.uk.

For Further Discussion

Chapter 1

1. On what issues do Marina Ottoway and Christopher Preble and Jason Logan disagree as to whether nation-building is justified? Whose ideas are most persuasive? Why?

2. John Chuckman, in his viewpoint, describes the death of a young Canadian soldier in Afghanistan. Does his story's message negate the ideas of John C. Hulsman and Alexis Y. Debat, who believe working with warlords is necessary and justified? Why or why not?

3. Max Borders uses a biological metaphor to make his argument that nation-building can transplant democratic institutions to foreign countries. Do you think biology is a good metaphor for nation-building? Why or why not?

Chapter 2

1. Patrick J. Donohoe believes the U.S. Army can train officers to be both warriors and nation-builders. What does he use to base that claim on and why? Do you find his book choice to be significant to the relationship between nation-building and global terrorism?

2. Representative Ron Paul gives two arguments why nation-building is a failing strategy against terrorism in two different viewpoints. What idea or ideas do you find behind both arguments? Are the ideas convincing?

Chapter 3

1. Donald H. Rumsfeld and Jason Yossef Ben-Meir argue that the Iraq nation-building project can work. Rumsfeld is former U.S. secretary of defense; Ben-Meir is a sociol-

ogy professor. Each of them has a different idea on how to make Iraq nation-building work. What are the differences? How might their different occupations affect their ideas on Iraq?

2. Ed Marek believes we should destroy U.S. enemies in Iraq, not nation-build. He comes from a military service background, as does former Secretary of Defense Donald H. Rumsfeld. How do their military worldviews differ as they relate to nation-building in Iraq? Why do you think that is?

Chapter 4

1. Peter Beinart and Jeffrey H. Fargo argue that nation-building provides hope for failed states, and bears repetition even when it fails. This would seem to be a money-losing, impoverished economic model that taxpayers and potential nation-building sponsors would not fund in the long term. What arguments do Beinart and Fargo give for repeating nation-building until it succeeds? Are they persuasive? Why or why not?

2. Matthew Riemer argues that indigenous ethnic differences may spoil nation-building imposed on them by outsiders. Robert McMahon discusses why United Nations nation-building may not be long-lasting. Where do their two viewpoints agree and disagree?

3. Jason M. Brownlee believes nation-building works best through small, modest projects. Seth G. Jones argues that securing health care is a key to nation-building success. Can these two ideas be joined together to create a successful model for 21st-century nation-building, in your opinion? Why or why not? Whose ideas do you find most important?

Organizations to Contact

The editors have compiled the following list of organizations concerned with the issues debated in this book. The descriptions are derived from materials provided by the organizations. All have publications or information available for interested readers. The list was compiled on the date of publication of the present volume; the information provided here may change. Be aware that many organizations take several weeks or longer to respond to inquiries, so allow as much time as possible.

Council on Foreign Relations

58 East Sixty-Eighth St., New York, NY   10021
(212) 434-9400 • fax: (212) 986-2984
e-mail: communications@cfr.org
Web site: www.cfr.org

The Council on Foreign Relations is a nonpartisan organization seeking to promote understanding of America's role in the world through its foreign policy. The council convenes forums on important issues, operates a think tank where prominent international affairs scholars can conduct research and write commissions books and reports, such as "Why We Should Plan to Pay for Nation-Building," and publishes *Foreign Affairs*, a journal of global politics.

Education for Peace in Iraq Center (EPIC)

1101 Pennsylvania Ave. SE, Washington, DC   20003
(202) 543-6176
Web site: www.epic-usa.org

The Education for Peace in Iraq Center is a nonprofit organization that seeks to promote policies and programs that benefit and support Iraqi citizens. The EPIC blog is updated daily to provide information from a wide variety of news sources, journals, and research publications. EPIC *Dispatches* is an online publication providing Iraqi analysis, field reports, and links to Iraqi sources. EPIC's *Iraq Forum* is a series of policy seminars on the Iraq situation. Audio transcripts are available on EPIC's Web site, including discussions such as "Iraqi Views on the Aftermath of War and Post-Conflict Reconstruction."

The Heritage Foundation

214 Massachusetts Ave. NE, Washington, DC   20002
(202) 546-4400 • fax: (202) 546-8328
e-mail: info@heritage.org
Web site: www.heritage.org

The Heritage Foundation is a research and educational institute dedicated to scholarship, formulation and promotion of conservative public policies. It publishes a variety of position papers and research articles on subjects deemed vital to America's interests and security, such as "Post-Conflict and Culture: Changing America's Military for 21st Century Missions."

Hoover Institution

Stanford University, Stanford, CA   94305-6010
(650) 423-1754 • fax: (650) 723-1687
e-mail: horaney@hoover.stanford.edu
Web site: www.hoover.stanford.edu

The Hoover Institution is a research center devoted to the advanced study of public policy, politics, economics, and international affairs. It publishes the quarterly *Hoover Digest* and *Policy Review*, a newsletter, and special reports, including articles such as "Can Iraq Become a Democracy?" and "War and Aftermath."

The Independent Institute

100 Swan Way, Suite 200, Oakland, CA   94621-1428
(510) 632-1366 • fax: (510) 568-6040
Web site: www.independent.org

The Independent Institute is a nonpartisan research and analysis, scholar-based organization, seeking to foster new and effective directions for the study of governance, and to provide solutions to its problems. The institute publishes *The Independent Review*, a quarterly journal; *The Lighthouse*, a weekly e-mail newsletter with articles like "Democratic Nation-Building and Political Violence;" books such as Ivan Eland's *The Emperor Has No Clothes: U.S. Foreign Policy Exposed*, challenging a U.S. policy of preemptive war and nation-building; policy reports; research papers; and *The Independent*, a quarterly newsletter.

Institute for War and Peace Reporting (IWPR)

48 Grays Inn Road, London   WC1X 8LT
  UK
+44 (0)20 7831 1030 • fax: +44 (0)20 7831 1050
Web site: www.iwpr.net

The Institute for War and Peace Reporting is a nonpartisan organization that promotes and sponsors initiatives to build and maintain local media in the midst of war, conflict, post-conflict, and reconstruction zones worldwide. IWPR also reports on and analyzes news. Some of its reports include the "Afghan Recovery Report" and the "Afghan Press Monitor."

The Institute of World Affairs (IWA)

1321 Pennsylvania Ave. SE, Washington, DC   20003
(202) 544-4141
e-mail: info@iwa.org
Web site: www.iwa.org

The Institute of World Affairs is a nonprofit, nonpartisan organization founded to foster conflict resolution and international understanding. The institute provides a variety of programs designed to prevent violence and construct postconflict peace-building. IWA supports seminars, lectures, and publications on conflict resolution, including *IWA e-Newsletters, Investigating Democracy Roundtable Series*, and other reports such as "Political Realities: The Diplomatic Process and Design of Peace-keeping Missions."

International Peace Research Institute (PRIO)
Hausmanns Gate 7, NO-0186, Oslo
  Norway
+47 22 54 77 00 • fax: +47 22 54 77 01
e-mail: info@prio.no
Web site: www.prio.no

The International Peace Research Institute focuses on scholar research and publication surrounding issues of violent conflict and transformational peace building. PRIO publishes books and articles including the forthcoming (as of 2007) "Building 'National' Armies—Building Nations? Determinants of Success for Post-Intervention Integration Efforts."

International Republican Institute (IRI)
1225 Eye St., NW, Suite 700, Washington, DC   20005
(202) 408-9450 • fax: (202) 408-9462
e-mail: info@iri.org
Web site: www.iri.org

The International Republican Institute is a nonpartisan, conservative organization promoting worldwide democracy through formation of political parties, civic institutions, democratic governance, and the rule of law. The IRI publishes brochures, newsletters, books, and articles such as "Spreading Democracy Is No Quick Fix, But It's Our Noble Duty," and "Why 'Soft Partition' of Iraq Won't Work."

Middle East Forum
1500 Walnut St., Suite 1050, Philadelphia, PA   19102
(215) 546-5406 • fax: (215) 546-5409
e-mail: info@meforum.org
Web site: www.meforum.org

The Middle East Forum is a think tank working to define and promote American interests in the Middle East. It supports American ties to Middle East democracies such as Israel and Turkey. Publisher of the policy-oriented *Middle East Quar-*

terly, which includes articles like "Will U.S. Democratization Policy Work? Democracy in the Middle East," its Web site includes articles, summaries of activities, and a discussion forum.

Middle East Institute

1761 N St. NW, Washington, DC   20036-2882
(202) 785-1141 • fax: (202) 331-8861
e-mail: mideasti@mideasti.org
Web site: www.themiddleeastinstitute.org

The institute's charter mission is to promote understanding of Middle Eastern cultures, languages, religions, and politics. It publishes books, research papers, audiotapes, videos, and transcripts from forums it convenes, such as the transcript from "Fractured Realities: A Middle East in Crisis Panel: Reconstructing Afghanistan and Iraq." The institute also publishes the quarterly *Middle East Journal*.

Middle East Media Research Institute (MEMRI)

PO Box 27837, Washington, DC   20038-7837
(202) 955-9070 • fax: (202) 955-9077
e-mail: memri@memri.org
Web site: www.memri.org

The Middle East Media Research Institute explores the Middle East through the region's media. MEMRI bridges the language gap that exists between the West and the Middle East, providing timely translations of Arabic, Persian, and Turkish media, and original analysis of political, ideological, intellectual, social, cultural, and religious trends in the Middle East. Its *Inquiry and Analysis* series offers commentary on topics such as, "Iraqi National Congress—an Exercise in Democracy."

Middle East Policy Council

1730 M St. NW, Suite 512, Washington, DC   20036-4505
(202) 396-6767 • fax: (202) 296-5791
e-mail: info@mepc.org
Web site: www.mepc.org

The Middle East Policy Council was founded in 1981 to expand public discussion and understanding of issues affecting U.S. policy in the Middle East. The council is a nonprofit, educational organization that operates nationwide. It publishes the quarterly *Middle East Policy Journal*, which includes articles such as Stephen Day's "Barriers to Federal Democracy in Iraq: Lessons from Yemen."

United Nations Development Programme for Iraq (UNDP in Iraq)

Communications Office, New York, NY   10017
(212) 906-5382 • fax: (212) 906-5364
e-mail: nadine.shamounki@undp.org
Web site: www.iq.undp.org

The United Nations Development Programme for Iraq seeks to help reconstruct the country through three main avenues: democratic governance, economic development and employment, and infrastructure construction. The UNDP in Iraq promotes these three areas through citizen participation in the civic process, gender and human rights building, and utilizing the expertise of Iraqi expatriates to rebuild their country. The UNDP Web site contains reports such as the "Iraq Living Conditions Survey 2004," and "Infrastructure and the Environment," a UNDP strategy to contribute to Iraq's reconstruction through rehabilitating and modernizing the infrastructure.

Bibliography of Books

Irwin Abrams and Wang Gungwu (eds.)
The Iraq War and Its Consequences: Thoughts of Nobel Peace Laureates and Eminent Scholars, World Scientific, 2003.

Scott Anderson
The Man Who Tried to Save the World: The Dangerous Life and Mysterious Disappearance of Fred Cuny, New York: Doubleday, 1999.

Joseph Baude
The New Iraq: Rebuilding the Country for Its People, the Middle East, and the World, New York: Basic Books, 2003.

Jane Boulden
Peace Enforcement: The United Nations Experience in Congo, Somalia, and Bosnia, Westport, CT: Praeger, 2001.

Kevin M. Cahill (ed.)
Human Security for All: A Tribute to Sergio Vieiva de Mello, New York: Fordham University Press, 2004.

Ivo Daalder, Nicole Gnesotto, and Philip Gordon (eds.)
Crescent of Crisis: U.S.–European Strategy for the Greater Middle East, Washington, DC: Brookings Institution Press European Institute for Security Studies, 2006.

Gary T. Dempsey with Roger W. Fontaine
Fool's Errand: America's Recent Encounters with Nation Building, Washington, DC: Cato Institute, 2001.

James Dobbins — *The Beginner's Guide to Nation-Building*, Santa Monica, CA: RAND, 2007.

James Dobbins — *America's Role in Nation Building: From Germany to Iraq*, Santa Monica, CA: RAND, 2003.

Toby Dodge — *Inventing Iraq: The Failure of Nation Building and a History Denied*, New York: Columbia University, 2003.

Antonio Donini (ed.) — *Nation Building Unraveled? Aid, Peace and Justice in Afghanistan*, Bloomfield, CT: Kumarian Press, 2004.

Noah Feldman — *What We Owe Iraq: War and the Ethics of Nation Building*, Princeton, NJ: Princeton University Press, 2004.

Francis Fukuyama (ed.) — *Nation-Building: Beyond Afghanistan and Iraq*, Baltimore: Johns Hopkins University Press, 2006.

Williams H. Garland — *Engineering Peace: The Military Role in Postconflict Reconstruction*, Washington, DC: United States Institute of Peace Press, 2005.

Raymond A. Hinnebusch — *The International Politics of the Middle East*, New York: Palgrave, 2003.

Michael Ignatieff — *Empire Lite: Nation Building in Bosnia, Kosovo, and Afghanistan*, Toronto: Penguin Canada, 2003.

Ray Salvatore Jennings	*The Road Ahead: Lessons in Nation Building from Japan, Germany, and Afghanistan for Postwar Iraq*, Washington, DC: United States Institute of Peace, 2003.
Gilles Kepel	*The War for Muslim Minds: Islam and the West*, Cambridge, MA: Belknap Press of Harvard University Press, 2004.
James Kitfield	*War and Destiny: How the Bush Revolution in Foreign and Military Affairs Redefined American Power*, Washington, DC: Potomac Books, 2005.
Nicholas N. Kittrie	*The Future of Peace in the Twenty-First Century: To Mitigate Domestic Discontents and Harmonize Global Diversity*, Durham, NC: Carolina Academic Press, 2003.
Kees Kooning	*Political Armies: The Military and Nation Building in the Age of Democracy*, New York: Zed Books, 2002.
Stephen Lanier	*Low Intensity Conflict and Nation-Building in Iraq: A Chronology*, Washington, DC: Center for Strategic and International Studies, 2004.
Alexander T. J. Lennon	*The Battle for Hearts and Minds: Using Soft Power to Undermine Terror Networks*, Boston: MIT Press, 2003.

Michael A. Morrison and Melinda S. Zook	*Revolutionary Currents: Nation Building in the Transatlantic World*, Lanham, MD: Rowman & Littlefield, 2004.
Greg Mortenson and David Oliver Relin	*Three Cups of Tea: One Man's Mission to Promote Peace, One School at a Time*, New York: Viking, Penguin, 2006.
Williamson Murray (ed.)	*A Nation at War in an Era of Strategic Change*, Carlisle Barracks, PA: U.S. Army War College, 2004.
Robert C. Orr (ed.)	*Winning the Peace: An American Strategy for Post-Conflict Reconstruction*, Washington, DC: CSIS Press, 2004.
Roland Paris	*At War's End: Building Peace after Civil Conflict*, New York: Cambridge University Press, 2004.
Robert Perito	*Where Is the Lone Ranger When We Need Him? America's Search for a Postconflict Stability Force*, Washington, DC: United States Institute of Peace Press, 2004.
Oliver P. Richmond and Henry F. Carey (eds.)	*Subcontracting Peace: The Challenges of the NGO Peacebuilding*, Ashgate, 2005.
William A. Rigby	*Nation Building: An Essential Army Task*, Carlisle Barracks, PA: U.S. Army War College, 2003.

Philip G. Roeder and Donald Rothchild — *Sustainable Peace: Power and Democracy after Civil Wars*, Ithaca, NY: Cornell University Press, 2005.

Jerry M. Rosenberg — *Nation-Building: A Middle East Recovery Program*, Lanham, MD: University Press of America, 2003.

Robert I. Rotberg — *When States Fail: Causes and Consequences*, Princeton, NJ: Princeton University Press, 2004.

Barnett R. Rubin — *Afghanistan's Uncertain Transition from Turmoil to Normalcy*, Washington, DC: Council on Foreign Relations, 2006.

Michael Seymour (ed.) — *The Fate of the Nation-State*, Montreal: McGill-Queen's University Press, 2004.

Cynthia Watson — *Nation-Building: A Reference Handbook*, Santa Barbara, CA: ABC-CLIO, 2004.

Index